TAUNTON'S
FRONT YARD
IDEA BOOK

TAUNTON'S FRONT YARD
IDEA BOOK

Jeni Webber

Principal photography by Lee Anne White

The Taunton Press

I dedicate this book to my dear parents, who inspired me as a child in the ways and gifts of the garden by showing me how to plant daffodils, encouraging me to pick bouquets for my teachers, and teaching me that willow branches stuck into moist earth become trees with care and time. Through it all, they taught me a reverence for nature and its mysteries and wove throughout this understanding a humble awareness of the connectivity of life.

Text © 2002 by Jeni Webber
Photographs except where noted © 2002 by Lee Anne White
Illustrations © 2002 by The Taunton Press, Inc.

 The Taunton Press
Inspiration for hands-on living®

The Taunton Press, Inc., 63 South Main Street, PO Box 5506,
Newtown, CT 06470-5506
e-mail: tp@taunton.com

Distributed by Publishers Group West

Editor: Lee Anne White
Jacket/Cover design: Carol Singer
Interior design: Carol Singer
Layout: Suzie Yannes
Illustrator: Jeni Webber
Photographer, except where noted: Lee Anne White

Library of Congress Cataloging-in-Publication Data
Webber, Jeni.
    Taunton's front yard idea book / Jeni Webber.
        p. cm.
    ISBN 1-56158-519-X
    1. Landscape gardening. I. Taunton Press. II. Title.

SB473 .W397 2002
712' .6--dc21   2002011520

Printed in the United States of America
10 9 8 7 6 5 4 3 2

Acknowledgments

First and foremost, I want to thank and acknowledge my editor, photographer, and friend, Lee Anne White. Without her continuous inspiration and dedication, this book would have simply remained a concept. Her way with a camera amazes me; I am always impressed by her ability to capture the essence of a garden. I can't thank Lee Anne enough for her friendship, craftsmanship, and generous assistance through all aspects of the project.

My longtime friend Anna Kondolf generously shared her expertise on lighting design. Anna contributed essential information and landscapes to shoot for the chapter on lighting. Her artful lighting illuminates many fine homes and businesses in the San Francisco Bay area.

While working on this book, I have met so many kind and inspiring people. I want to thank all the homeowners who shared their homes and their stories and allowed us to photograph their gardens. I am very grateful to the many designers who helped us find front yards for inclusion in the book.

My aunt Sydney Eddison is a woman who always either has dirt on her hands or her hands on a keyboard. A dedicated and talented gardener and writer who has shown me what one can create and accomplish in a lifetime, she has both inspired and encouraged me along the way.

I would also like to thank the many wonderful individuals who have supported me through the years, inspired me in the ways of creativity, and encouraged me to follow my dreams: my high school art teacher Jack Bledsoe; my dear friends Susan Corfman, Barbara Guarino, and Jayme Martinez; my brother Russ Webber; my family in Yorkshire, England; Bev Thorne, his sons, and my colleagues at the design studio; and many other friends too numerous to mention by name. I'd like to acknowledge the many designers, past and present, whose work has become my library. And last, but not least, I want to thank my clients for their warm encouragement while I was working on this book and for allowing me to use their land as a canvas for learning.

Contents

Introduction

Wherever you go in America, the houses and landscapes look so familiar. In the last half-century or so, houses were mass-produced, and front-yard landscapes were simplified to little more than a lawn, a few evergreen shrubs, and perhaps a specimen tree or two so that they could be installed quickly and affordably.

Although this long-standing lawn-and-foundation-shrub model may have been good for developers, it has done little to enhance the residential landscape. Instead, it has resulted in a homogenous landscape in which it is difficult to tell one home from the next, and where families spend less time than ever before in their own front yards. It has also had serious environmental consequences. Lawns, though they certainly have their benefits as open spaces or as play areas, have greatly reduced the natural habitat for far too many species of plants and animals. They have also been forced on regions that cannot naturally support them due to seasonal patterns of rainfall or other environmental constraints.

When lawns were first introduced, yard maintenance was based on an organic model of farming and gardening. Compost and marsh sludge were applied seasonally to lawns; weeds were tolerated or pulled by hand; sheep took care of mowing; and rainfall supplied all the water needed. Since then, however, we've raised the standards for lawns—putting up with fewer weeds and requiring a more manicured appearance. As a result, we've developed a strong dependence on chemical fertilizers, herbicides, and pesticides, and frequent irrigation has begun to strain many local water sources. Rainwater runoff is riddled with these chemicals and has become a major source of pollution in our waterways.

New Trends in Landscape Design

Fortunately, times are changing. Individual homeowners, entire neighborhoods, and even many developers have begun to realize the personal and environmental benefits, as well as cost-effectiveness, of designing more suitable front-yard landscapes. Lawns are getting smaller and, in many cases, have been replaced by alternative ground covers and native plants. Homeowners are also beginning to use their front yards again and are finding creative and socially acceptable ways to distinguish their homes from those of their neighbors while still fitting them into the surrounding landscape. In many cities, front-yard gardens are now almost commonplace.

There are also new types of residential communities being developed. Narrow, tree-lined streets keep these neighborhoods cooler, and natural drainage swales reduce the amount of water carried away in storm drains and make that water more readily available to plants. A network of pathways and shared green spaces support neighborhood activities—everything from potluck dinners to baseball games. Front porches and courtyards serve as outdoor rooms for reading, dining, and visiting with neighbors. It is a pleasure to wander through these neighborhoods—to see the diversity of plantings, discover homes with personality, and see children playing games and people sitting on their porches.

It only takes one person to make a difference. I've seen it in the landscaping projects

I've been involved with, and in the dozens of neighborhoods across the country that we visited while creating this book. As soon as one homeowner updates a front yard, others follow suit.

In this book, I hope you'll find some new ways to think about front yards, as well as practical, hands-on advice for dealing with everything from foundation plantings and parking spaces to designing spaces for family activities. May it spark your imagination so that you can start a new revolution to reclaim the front yards in your neighborhood.

Getting Started

For too many years, front yards have been the misfits of the landscape. What started off as utilitarian spaces in the founding days of our country were transformed into something quite ornamental by the mid-1800s. But after World War II, when the housing boom hit the suburbs, front yards became, well, boring. Now, in the early years of a new century, front yards are finally getting the attention they deserve. After all, the front yard is the first thing you see when you pull up in front of your house—whether you own many acres or a tiny plot of land. It can cloak your home with warmth and personality.

With the rising cost of real estate, it makes perfect sense to make the most of this space. In fact, any real estate agent will tell you about the importance of curb appeal when it's time to sell your home. But you should landscape for your own enjoyment, not for potential buyers. When you keep

this in mind, the front yard should do three things:

- Visually tie your house to the surrounding landscape, giving your home personality and a sense of place
- Create a welcoming environment
- Serve your family's needs—whether for outdoor activities, parking, or entertaining guests

▲A carefully crafted stone wall softened by lush plantings marks a driveway entry.

◀A landscape that matures gracefully requires planning. Shrubs should be sited so that they can grow naturally to their full stature. Pathways should enhance logical circulation patterns. Views should be envisioned before trees are cut or planted.

▲**Semipublic spaces are unique. Because they are yours, they should reflect your personality** and be places you can enjoy. Because they are constantly on view to others, they should be designed with more restraint than a back yard might be. The goal is not to make your yard look like your neighbors'; it's to make it look cared for and in keeping with the surrounding landscape and architecture.

In many ways, landscaping a front yard is much like decorating a room in your house. You want to convey a sense of style; make good use of shape, texture, and your favorite colors; and arrange all the elements so they are both functional and inviting. But outdoors, you have a few new elements to add to the equation. First of all, front yards are semipublic spaces. You may own the land, but your yard is part of a neighborhood and a broader regional landscape. While it's important to distinguish your landscape from others, it also has to blend in. In addition, you'll be working with plants, which add a living element to the design palette. Not only do plants grow over time but they change throughout the seasons. Though working with plants is a little more complex than working with fabrics and paints, I believe it's what makes landscaping exciting.

Some of you will be starting with a blank slate—a bare patch of land in front of a new home. Others will be updating existing landscapes. In either case, you'll start at the same place. Before you go shopping for plants or supplies, you need to consider the following:

- **Site**—the physical terrain, your neighborhood, and the regional landscape in which you live
- **Space**—how you desire to use your front yard, what you want it to look like, and how you want to feel when you are in it
- **Budget**—how much time and money you have to invest, and whether you will do the work yourself or hire professionals to help with the job
- **Schedule**—the time frame you have for realizing your goals (whether immediate or long term) and what you consider your priorities
- **Maintenance**—how much time and money you want to spend maintaining your landscape

We'll look at all of these issues in a broad sense in this chapter, and in more detail throughout the book. But by taking time to address them up front, you will come up with some basic principles to guide you through the landscape design process.

▼**It can be difficult to create both a place** to garden and a lawn where growing children can play, especially on a busy street. Here, the picket fence makes the yard safe for play while serving as the backdrop for a perennial border. The fancifully detailed arbor echoes architectural elements of the home.

A Color-Coordinated Landscape

If the soul is in the details, there's plenty of soul in this front yard. It's not a very big yard, but it's certainly worth exploring. At first glance, you'll notice a rhapsody of earthy colors—from the aubergine-colored house with silky brown curtains to the terra-cotta pots, soft-toned stonework, and wine-foliaged foundation plants. Then the lush plantings, which create a frame within which to view the house, will pique your interest. And finally, upon closer inspection, you'll find the intricate details of the stonework will capture your fancy— from the artfully crafted retaining walls, paths, and steps to a curbside landing strip and a pebble-mosaic water feature where homeowner Tim O'Hearn sits with his son to feed the fish.

Landscape designer and artist Jeffrey Bale is the mastermind behind this creation. He started by terracing what was once a small, sloped lawn to create flat planting beds filled with flowering shrubs, perennials, ornamental grasses, and bulbs. He color-coordinated the house, hardscaping, and plantings and created a focal point with the water feature—which doubles as front-yard seating. Because the area is loosely enclosed by flowering shrubs, it makes a wonderful gathering place at the end of a busy day.

▲**Plantings neatly frame the view of this home's entry, while creating comfortable surroundings** that enable the homeowners to enjoy their front yard.

◄A low retaining wall can transform a sloped yard into a flat one—whether it's used for lawn or plantings. This one is as artful as it is practical.

▲The gentle splash of a water feature can help drown out distracting neighborhood noise to create a soothing setting. This pebble-mosaic water feature was designed with built-in seating walls where friends and family can gather in the evening.

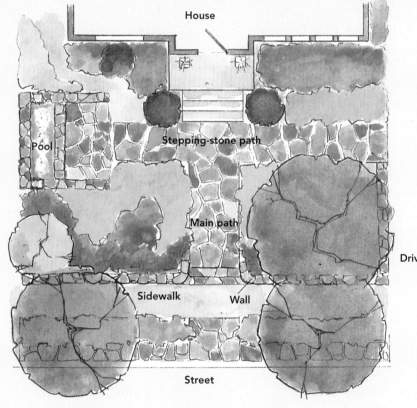

House

Pool

Stepping-stone path

Main path

Driveway

Sidewalk   Wall

Street

►**You can easily enhance** your view from inside by adding a focal point. Here, a large container planting draws the eye.

Take Stock of Your Situation

Whenever I take on a new landscaping job for a client, I first have to take stock of the situation; as a homeowner, you should do the same. Allow some time for this. Get out a notepad and pencil, and involve your entire family in the process. Even though you may be anxious to start digging, it's important not to rush this first crucial step.

Start by sizing up your site. You may love your house and property—and hopefully, you do—but you still need to take a good, close look at it with a critical eye. There are 10 steps to this process that involve different ways of looking at your yard. To help you through this process, I've included a list of questions to ask as you evaluate your front yard from different points of view (see the sidebar on the facing page). Jot down any observations and ideas on your notepad as you do this.

It's a good idea to make a scale drawing of your site while you're at it. You don't have to be an artist—just handy with a tape measure and ruler (see the sidebar on p. 12). With several photocopies of a site plan, you can make notes about light patterns, aspect (which way your house faces), existing plants, problem areas, and other observations on this "map" of your property. A site plan will also serve as the basis for your landscape plan.

A landscape plan allows you to play around with ideas and change your mind without pulling out the garden tools—to go from wildly impractical dreams to workable solutions before you dig the first hole or lay the first brick. A plan also helps when there are two or more interested parties—perhaps you and a spouse or other family members— as you can more amicably work out solutions to your differing needs and desires. And a plan lets you place plants thoughtfully, keeping in mind how large they'll grow over time.

How to Evaluate Your Site

To evaluate your site, follow these steps:

1. Look out your windows and doors. Are there views to screen? Can others see into your house? Would you like to create views of gardens or children's play areas?

2. Look at your house from the street. What's your general impression? Is there a clear path to the door? Are plants overgrown or growing against the house? What architectural elements do you wish to accent or screen?

3. Walk around your front yard. How is the space shaped? Where do you need paths? Are steps loose and wobbly? Is there a place for a comfortable chair?

4. Notice how you feel in your yard. Is it too open or exposed, or do you feel claustrophobic? Do you want more or less privacy?

5. Look at the land. Is it flat, sloped, or rolling? Damp or dry? What kind of soil do you have? Does it drain well after a heavy rain?

6. Inspect existing plantings. Are they healthy and attractive, or do certain plants need to be pruned, moved, or removed? Do they offer seasonal interest? Do you have enough variety in plantings? Or perhaps too much variety?

7. Look at how the light falls on your property. Do you have full sun, heavy shade, something in between, or a mix? Do you need to create more shade or open up the site to create more sunlight? Which direction does your house face?

8. Think about your local weather patterns. Does your house need to be screened from strong winter winds? Should your paths be easy to shovel in snow? Would a breezeway between the house and garage keep you dry in the rainy season?

9. Stop and listen. Do you hear the pleasant sounds of chirping birds or children's laughter? Do you need to buffer sounds from passing cars?

10. Drive around your neighborhood and the surrounding countryside. What plants, construction materials, and landscaping styles distinguish your region from other parts of the country? What landscaping ideas do you like that would be right for your site?

11. Evaluate your property at night. Do paths and steps need to be better illuminated? Can you see to back up your car? Is there a glare that needs to be screened?

▲ **This corner lot had little back yard,** so a play space was created out front. It features screening for safety, a lawn for activities, and a kid-sized fort for quiet moments.

Sketching a Site Plan

Site plans aren't difficult to draw, but you do need accurate measurements. Start by roughly sketching your property boundaries, your house, and any significant structures on a large sheet of paper. You can write the measurements on this plan as you go. Keep in mind that you're only working with the front yard, so that's all you need to show. Stake the corners of your property and measure the distance between them with a long tape measure. Next, measure your house. To place the house in relation to the property boundaries, measure from each corner of the house perpendicularly (two directions) to the property boundary. Next, add any driveways, paths, or other structures. It's also a good idea to show existing planting beds, paths, and trees.

Once you have your measurements, make a scale drawing on paper with a ruler, T-square, and drafting triangle. A three-sided architect's ruler will easily convert your measurements to scale. To determine your working scale, divide the length of your property by the working length of the paper. For instance, to draw a 100-foot property line in a 25-inch space, you'll work in ¼-inch scale (¼- and ⅛-inch scale are the most commonly used).

Start by drawing the house to scale, then systematically place the other elements of the page—starting with the property lines and moving on to other structures, hardscaping, and, finally, any plantings. If something looks out of place, you can always go outside and check your measurements. Once you've finished, make several photocopies for playing around with different design ideas. Tracing paper also works well for experimenting with ideas.

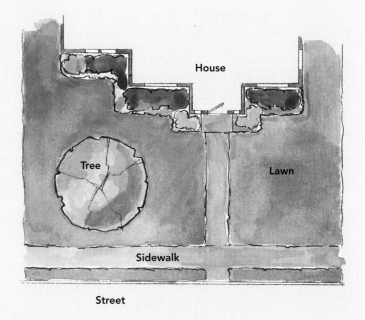

Landscape design is a practical, intuitive, and creative process. An effective design weaves together family needs and interests, architectural elements, plantings, and landforms into a synergistic whole. No single solution suits any one site or family, and certainly, no single solution suits all the homes in a neighborhood. I once thought that landscape design was the fine art of compromise—identifying and including only things that everyone could agree upon. Over the years, however, I've realized that's just designing to the lowest common denominator, and the results are rarely good. Unless you're the only person living in your house, talk it over with the others. You can almost always include something for everyone.

◀ **It's your space, so use it.** Instead of a stoop, this home-owner created a deck out front. Because it is discreetly screened from the road, it's an ideal place for enjoying dinner or a game of cards.

▼ **This toddler's play space was tucked neatly** into a corner that was screened from the street by a hedge but could be easily viewed from the house. It uses gray chipped gravel instead of white sand, and, edged by an elegant pathway and herbs, this space blends right in with other landscape elements.

Make the Most of Your Space

A front yard should be designed for those who live there. It must be functional as well as attractive. You need a place to park your car and a convenient route for hauling arm-loads of groceries to the kitchen. If someone in your home is handicapped, he or she must be able to get around easily. If you have young children or pets and live on a busy street, an enclosed space will help ensure their safety.

The front yard is often an excellent place for activities. When doing things in your front yard, you'll begin to feel more in touch with your community. It's nice to see other people in a neighborhood, even if you don't know them well. This is especially true for

people with reduced mobility. Some of the activities you might consider include gardening, relaxing, entertaining, dining, recreation and games, washing the car, and more.

◄ **Trouble spots can become treasured spaces.** With a separate garage built into the front hillside, the owners transformed the rooftop into a terrace for gardening. In nice weather, they can also bring out patio furniture.

▼ **Think beyond the box.** Instead of straight courtyard walls, this homeowner added an interesting curve to create an outdoor dining area.

Consider practical needs too. Some households get by with one small car; others need space for an assortment of cars, trucks, sport utility vehicles, boats, and campers. Parking, in fact, is a major element in many front landscapes. Vehicles are wider and families have more cars per household than ever before. For this reason, most new homes have wider driveways, multiple-bay garages, turnaround slots, and expanded parking areas. Older landscapes are often renovated to widen driveways and add extra parking slots.

Every house has its own unique set of circumstances that must be addressed in the landscape planning process. If you live on a hill, you may need to improve access or solve erosion and runoff problems. Perhaps you live in a neighborhood where safety or security is an issue, or maybe you just prefer your privacy. Do you live on an exposed mountainside where the wind rattles your windows in winter, or in the middle of a

field where the sun bakes your house in summer? Along busy urban and suburban streets, you may need to design walls and hedges to help lessen the impact of traffic noise. On small lots, you may need a fence or other screening for privacy. And if you

▲**Study your architecture. The formal, symmetric design of this colonial home** dictated balanced, clipped shrubs; a period-style fence painted to match the house trim; and a central path of brick to complement the house façade.

have a steep lot, you'll need easy access to your home as well as hillside landscaping that requires very little upkeep.

Take Cues from Your Architecture

One of the best places to look for inspiration is your house. The style of your house will, to a large degree, dictate the style of your landscape, whether formal, informal, or contemporary. The shape of your house, whether tall, boxy, or horizontal, should be echoed in many of the plants you choose. Architectural features—such as doors, bay windows, or porches—are elements to be

either emphasized or downplayed with landscaping. The relationship between entries and parking areas will signal where paths should be laid.

Often, there are architectural elements or building materials that can be used throughout the landscape—split-rail fencing with a natural wood home; a brick path leading to a home with a brick foundation; a matching stucco courtyard wall surrounding the entry of a stucco house; Victorian wood trim details echoed in arbors or fence posts. Colors can also be repeated or contrasted in a complementary way—both with construction materials and plantings.

Landscape Elements Common to Architectural Styles

For a unified look, it helps to include landscape elements that suit the style of your home. Here are some common planting, hardscaping, and decorative elements to consider for different types of architecture.

COTTAGE
- Picket fences—all styles and colors
- Geometric beds with a profusion of plants
- Little or no lawn
- Mix of flowers, herbs, and vegetables
- Often eclectic or personalized style
- Painted-wood or wrought-iron garden furniture

COLONIAL
- Picket fences and clipped hedges (especially boxwood)
- Brick paths
- Symmetric plantings
- Geometric beds
- Classic teak garden furniture

VICTORIAN
- Usually symmetric plantings
- Colorful bedding schemes and window boxes
- Elaborate details in house, fences, arbors, and gazebos
- Wrought-iron garden furniture

CAPE COD
- Usually symmetric plantings
- Small lawn
- Simple plantings and window boxes
- Naturally weathered or painted wooden garden furniture
- Stone walls and paths

CRAFTSMAN BUNGALOW
- Symmetric or asymmetric plantings, depending on house design
- Layered, naturalistic plantings
- Small lawn
- Detailed hardscaping, often with a mix of brick, wood, and stone
- Wooden garden furniture with simple lines
- Front porches and terraces

MEDITERRANEAN
- Symmetric or asymmetric plantings, depending on house design
- Little or no lawn
- Mediterranean herbs and plants with silver foliage
- Stucco walls, often draped in brightly colored vines

▲Architectural lines of the house are picked up in the lamppost.

- Tile and cut-stone pavers
- Often with terracing and water features

SOUTHWESTERN
- Often asymmetric plantings
- Succulents and other drought-tolerant plants
- Little or no lawn
- Gravel ground covers; tile and sandstone pavers
- Stucco or adobe walls
- Heavy, carved wooden garden furniture

ENGLISH/COUNTRY
- Usually symmetric plantings
- Large expanses of lawn (may be mown or natural)
- Extensive use of mixed beds and borders
- Flagstone and brick used for walls, paths, and terraces
- Prominent but simply designed garden features (arbors, pergolas)
- Teak or heavy wrought-iron garden furniture

RUSTIC
- Symmetric or asymmetric plantings, depending on house style
- Naturalistic plantings—often with natives or in a woodland setting
- Split-rail fences
- Adirondack, primitive, or weathered garden furniture
- Stone, gravel, and mulched paths

FARMHOUSE
- Often symmetric plantings
- Large shade trees close to house
- Larger lawns, meadows, or naturalistic ground covers
- Loose foundation plantings, usually with some perennials or bulbs mixed in
- Picket, split-rail, or cattle fencing
- Brick and stepping-stone paths
- Simple painted garden furniture

▲**Distinctive plantings and decorative items** carry out an Asian theme.

CONTEMPORARY
- Usually asymmetric plantings
- Extensive use of lawns and evergreens
- Stained or weathered garden furniture
- Flagstone paths and low walls

POSTMODERN
- Usually asymmetric plantings—simple, yet bold
- Little or no lawn; highly manicured where the lawn exists
- Geometric planting beds and hardscaped areas
- Often without foundation plantings
- Courtyard entries with sculptures
- Metal, glass, and concrete materials
- Metal, contemporary, or artistic garden furniture

JAPANESE
- Usually asymmetric but regularly pruned plantings
- Mix of geometric and naturalistic paths
- Extensive use of evergreens and flowering trees—emphasis on plant form
- Color used subtly
- Symbolic use of stone, water, and earth
- Stone or wooden garden benches
- Boulders used for accent

◀This corner bench was built into a retaining wall. It serves as an invitation to neighbors to stop and visit with one another and to enjoy the homeowner's garden.

▼This Victorian farmhouse has an inviting front porch and is surrounded by lush plantings. Though most of the plantings—boxwood, hydrangeas, heavenly bamboo, and Lenten rose—are common in temperate climates, the hardy palm gives this setting a tropical feel.

Keeping in mind that front yards are semipublic spaces, it's a good idea to review any subdivision covenants before getting too far into the planning process to make sure you are aware of any restrictions. And though your yard doesn't have to look just like all the others on your street—in fact, it shouldn't—you do want to make sure that in a traditional neighborhood, you don't make changes too quickly or radically. For instance, it's usually easier to begin by expanding foundation plantings, resurfacing paths, and adding mailbox plantings than by constructing tall walls or converting manicured lawns to meadows.

The oft-quoted English poet and literary critic Alexander Pope wrote as long ago as the 1700s about "consulting the genius of a place" as you landscape. That just means designing a landscape that looks and feels at home—created in response to the specific terrain, environmental conditions, history, architecture, and inhabitants of a place. When you drive around your neighborhood and the countryside, look at things with a fresh eye. What gives your region a sense of

◀**A casual setting suits this informal house.** Large stone slabs serve as steps to the front door. The lawn, which would have been difficult to mow on this slope, was replaced with a mix of evergreen and deciduous plants. Teak chairs offer a place to sit and enjoy the garden.

uniqueness? Is it certain plants, a particular building style, or common landscaping materials? By incorporating some of those elements in your front yard, you gain the ability to vary the other elements while your landscape continues to fit in.

Designing a Master Plan

Armed with your site evaluation, list of ideas, and several copies of your site plan, it's time to begin thinking about the space and how it will be used. Details—such as

what kind of stone you want for the retaining wall or which shrubs to use in foundation plantings—come later. For now, just focus on the big picture.

I like to start with what landscape designers call a "bubble diagram." It's where you draw loose circles on your site plan around areas based on how you plan to use them. For example, you might draw a circle in a shady area for sitting, in a flat area for a patch of lawn, next to the side door for parking, or in a sunny spot for a garden. Include practical things too—like a place for the trash cans on pickup day or im-

► **This courtyard is intimate, not private.** The low wall doubles as seating so the owners can visit with their neighbors. Notice how the wall height varies at the corner, and how the tiles are laid at an angle to the wall for a subtle visual effect.

Bubble Diagram

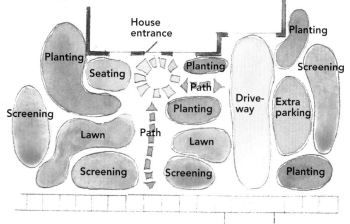

ing area? Or do you need a series of paths to get around easily?

Next, try your hand at sketching what you think the design might look like—the lawn, the paths, parking, sitting areas, and such. Draw up several different approaches, and get some feedback from other family members. Don't worry about your drawing skills. The point is to think through the changes on paper before you begin making them in the yard. It's much easier to redraw something that doesn't work than it is to move a path, dig up a plant, or reseed the lawn.

proved access from the garage to the kitchen door. Look back over your notes, and draw some more circles to mark areas where you need screening or more sun or that are too steep to mow. Think about how these spaces relate to each other and how you would get from one area to another. Did you just place the trash cans next to a seat-

Budgets, Schedules, and Priorities

Budgets and schedules go hand in hand. Few of us are blessed with unlimited financial resources. As a result, we tend to scale back our plans to what our current budget allows, rather than thinking about what's ideal for our property. I'd like to encourage you to think in a long-term way about your landscape. Just because you're thinking about the finished landscape doesn't mean that you have to install it all at once. By installing a landscape in phases, you can better manage your expenses and, if you like, do much of the hands-on work yourself. In the end, you'll be much more satisfied with the results.

Lawns, trees, and certain hardscaping features like patios or retaining walls are usually installed first. Lawns give children a place to play and provide a ground cover to prevent erosion. Trees need the longest time to get established. And for logistical reasons, many hardscaping features must be installed before gardens can be planted. It's also important to take care of grading projects early in the process, and to install any utilities—

▲ **You can save money while you help save the environment.** This retaining wall is built from broken concrete.

Native Flora for a Southwest Landscape

When landscape designer Carrie Nimmer starting digging up struggling front lawns in one of Phoenix's historic districts, she raised more than a few eyebrows. Pristine lawns were the pride of the neighborhood, but they weren't an appropriate ground cover in a region that receives fewer than 8 inches of rainfall a year. She replaced her lawn and that of two neighbors with drought-tolerant succulents and native wildflowers that flourish in the surrounding Saguaro desert.

Yet there's more to Carrie's approach to designing landscapes than replacing lawns with native plants. She also believes in creating inviting spaces. That's why she ripped out her concrete driveway, replaced it with ochre-toned chipped gravel, and

▲ **Succulents, cacti, and desert wildflowers** now thrive where lawn once languished. The seductively curving path issues an invitation to explore the garden.

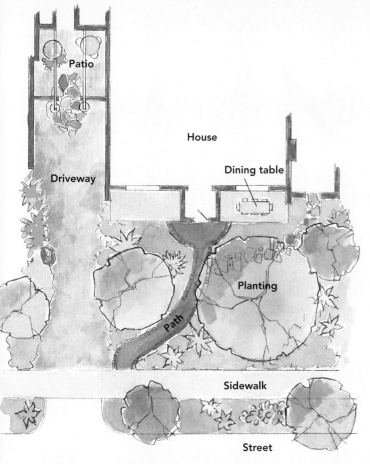

◀**Once a garage, now a cozy courtyard.** Concrete paving was replaced with dry-laid flagstone and pea gravel—which is both more permeable and better looking.

▲**A large outdoor table** is tucked into a terraced alcove not far from the front door, creating a place to dine, work, and gather with friends.

allowed plantings to soften the edges. In the evening, she can roll out the barbecue grill and transform the area into an outdoor patio where she sips wine with neighbors and watches children skate, bike, and play ball nearby.

With the help of her husband, Peter, an architect, she transformed the garage into a dramatic courtyard with a water feature and seating for two. And for larger gatherings, mesquite trees and other plantings provide screening for a dining area on a patio not far from the front door.

Patio

House

Driveway

Dining table

Planting

Path

Sidewalk

Street

Hiring a Design Professional

Landscape design is both an art and a science, drawing on the fields of design, horticulture, and construction. That's why it often makes sense to hire a professional—either for an overall concept plan, construction details, planting plans, installation, or all of the above. Whether you hire a landscape architect, landscape designer, or garden designer depends on your individual needs.

If you are situating a new home on a lot, installing a driveway, or rebuilding your front stoop, a landscape architect may be your best choice. Make sure you find one who specializes in residential design, as many landscape architects handle only commercial or municipal projects. Most states license landscape architects, who have generally attained advanced degrees in their field. Many are members of the American Society of Landscape Architects (ASLA).

Most landscape designers are not licensed, although they may have studied design or horticulture and be certified by the Association of Professional Landscape Designers (APLD). As a group, they tend to specialize in residential design and can help you create a master plan, address specific problems in your landscape, and install plantings.

Garden designers, who tend to focus more on creating gardens and working with plants than on overall landscape plans, don't have a governing body or membership organization. However, a garden designer may be just what you need for a small-scale project.

Ask to see examples of their work and check their references. Find out whether their specialty is space planning, hardscaping, or working with plants. Ask about the services they provide and how they bill for them. Most, but not all, will draw up concept plans, especially if there are hardscaping details. Some have their own crews and supervise the installation; others work with contractors; a few provide only design services and let you handle the installation. You can find design professionals in the Yellow Pages, by asking at local nurseries, by calling the ASLA or APLD, or by asking for referrals from homeowners with landscapes you admire.

such as outdoor lighting or irrigation systems. I also like to get a head start on amending the soil for any beds and borders.

One trick I've learned is to figure out where you'll get the most bang for your buck. In a front yard, that's often a new path to the front door, courtyard walls, updated foundation plantings, or a spruced-up entry. Driveway improvements, secondary paths, garden areas, and ornamental accents can be dealt with in subsequent years. Until you can invest in other plantings, vines will quickly and inexpensively give your place a lived-in look as they cover fences, walls,

◀**Instead of traditional foundation plantings,** this house sports raised beds filled with rich garden soil. A garden designer lives here, and he enjoys changing the bulbs and annuals for spectacular seasonal displays.

◀**If you're on a limited budget and want to spread** your landscaping out over several years, focus on your main path first. This one zigzags its way to the front door and is wide enough for a couple of chairs where the owners can enjoy watching the sunset.

and arbors, or are trained up and around windows and doorways.

Depending on your time, interests, and abilities, and the complexity of your site, you can either do the design work yourself or hire a professional to help. If you have a small yard and fairly simple plans and are reasonably handy, you may be able to tackle the entire project yourself. But for challeng-

ing sites or plans that call for lots of hardscaping elements such as terraces, retaining walls, parking courts, or steps, it's often a good idea to hire a landscape architect or landscape designer to draw up detailed plans, even if you want to serve as your own contractor or do much of the installation yourself.

2

Entries

Details like these eye-catching house numbers make a difference.

The front entry—whether a porch, stoop, landing, or courtyard—is the gateway to your home. It's here that you meet and greet visitors and see them off after a good visit. It's where you want them to pause and feel welcomed or to linger just a bit longer before leaving.

What does your front entry look like? Is it warm and inviting for those who wait at the door, or is it a cramped, stark environment with little to please the eye? Small details count for much here—a freshly painted door, a shiny brass knob, a colorful gathering of container plantings. Is there a roof to provide cover from rain and a convenient place to leave packages? Do the steps and paving complement your home? Are your house numbers visible from the street, and can guests find their way to the door safely and easily after dark?

At a minimum, entries offer a place to wait after someone knocks on your door. Yet they have the potential to be so much more—gathering places just waiting to be transformed into outdoor rooms. Expand a stoop or landing, and it becomes a terrace that can also be used for dining or entertaining. Hang some planted baskets and a swing on your porch, and it beckons you to relax with a glass of lemonade and a good book. Enclose your entry and you have an intimate courtyard setting perfect for dining, relaxing, or gardening.

◄**Plants soften hard surfaces, whether they are grown in pots, trained along eaves,** or allowed to spill over onto pathways. Here, manicured boxwood topiaries mix with a gently draping evergreen clematis to create a semiformal entry. The combination of architecture, plantings, and teal paint leads easily to the door.

► **Express yourself at the door.** Paint, hardware, plantings, and ornamental accents can all be used to convey personality. Here, it's clear that an artist and gardener lives within.

When you compose your landscape, make your front door the primary focal point. Most traditional homes are designed with the front door as the dominant feature. On many other houses, however, the garage may be more prominent or the entry may be obscured. When the front door is not the dominant focal point, strong visual cues such as lighted pathways or eye-catching containers placed at bends in the path are often needed to guide the way.

The architectural symmetry of your house is a good starting point. A symmetrically designed house calls for a symmetrical arrangement of objects or plantings on either side of the front door. For instance, you may have matching sconces, identical plantings, the same number of rocking chairs or matching box planters on either side of the door. Asymmetrical designs—those in which the front door is not centered on the house façade—need a different approach. What you place on either side of the door may be balanced, but it doesn't necessarily match. You may have a small deciduous tree, small evergreen shrub, and perennials on one side, balanced by a cluster of medium-sized evergreen shrubs on the other.

▲ **The two conical evergreen shrubs add a subtle sense of formality** to this otherwise informal, asymmetric entry. Flowering rhododendrons and pieris offer year-round interest with evergreen foliage and spring blossoms.

Stoops and Landings

The most common entries are stoops and landings. The only real difference between the two is their height. Landings are paved surfaces at or just above ground level, while stoops are raised, with two or more steps. Because they are raised, most stoops also have some sort of railing for safety. Stoops and landings may be covered with an awning or portico; local weather conditions are usually the driving factor behind these coverings. Because they provide shelter from rain and snow, they are more common in areas that receive ample precipitation than in arid regions. But even where the weather isn't a factor, awnings and porticos can help define an entry.

Another alternative for shelter—and one that is easy to add—is an arbor. Though an arbor won't keep you dry in a rainstorm, it can offer shade and wind protection, as well as add dimension, to your entry. Baskets of flowering plants can be hung from arbors, and colorful vines can be allowed to scramble up their sides and spill over the top. By planting several vines that flower in different seasons, you can enjoy color from spring through fall, or all year long in mild climates. Fragrant vines are a bonus for those passing through an arbor. If you don't have an arbor but want to achieve a similar effect, simply train vines up and over your doorway on a trellis or wire.

With a little patience, you can also create an attractive overhead canopy with trees. Your choice of trees is important, as they will be planted close to the house and your front path. Choose varieties that will not grow taller than about 25 feet (to prevent large branches from falling on your roof), with a more upright rather than a spreading canopy

▲ Color-coordinated accents like this awning draw attention. Instead of growing a wisteria (which can get unruly) over her door, the owner had an artist paint one that flowers year-round and never needs pruning.

Big Ideas Transform a Tiny Entry

You don't need a big entry to make a memorable impression. Anna and Verne Davis's entry is slightly recessed and located at the corner of their house. Despite its somewhat unlikely location, Atlanta garden designer Brooks Garcia has called attention to the area with attractive plantings and a cozy seating area.

To begin, he created an enclosed terrace surrounded by plantings on the front, a stone retaining wall on the side, and a green moon gate that leads to Anna's garden in the back yard. Vines soften the walls of the house and retaining wall, while loose plantings screen views and an unfortunately placed utility box, and an iron bench offers a place to sit. Small containers filled with succulents, geraniums, and other favorite flowers accent the area nicely, and a statuary dog stands sentinel, as if to offer fresh bouquets to arriving guests.

▲Though the entry is recessed, plantings and a pathway clearly point the way to this front door. The cluster of small ornamental trees also screens a utility box.

◄Place interesting details where they can be viewed up close. This succulent-filled container is right next to the front door.

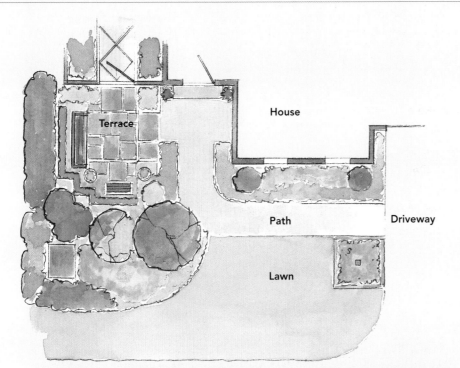

Terrace

House

Path

Driveway

Lawn

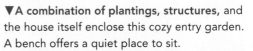

▼A combination of plantings, structures, and the house itself enclose this cozy entry garden. A bench offers a quiet place to sit.

▲ **A clematis-covered arbor** highlights this entry.

and with a deep root system that won't cause your path or foundation to buckle. The smaller maples (*Acer* spp.), crape myrtles (*Lagerstroemia* spp.), and shadblow (*Amelancier canadensis*) are all good selections.

Though typically small, stoops and landings have long been gathering spots. A couple of chairs or a bench are ideal for sitting a spell. If your space is tight, a chair or bench isn't even necessary as long as you have a few steps. Widened into a terrace, a stoop or landing takes on the character of an outdoor room, with seating space for a family or even a table and chairs for outdoor dining.

Vines to Train Around Doors

EVERGREEN VINES

Carolina jessamine (*Gelsemium sempervirens*)
Chilean jasmine (*Mandevilla laxa*)
Evergreen clematis (*Clematis armandii*)
Honeysuckle (*Lonicera* spp.)
Jasmine (*Jasminum polyanthum*)
Star jasmine (*Trachelospermum jasminoides*)
Wintercreeper (*Euonymous fortunei* var. *radicans*)

DECIDUOUS VINES

American bittersweet (*Celastrus scandens*)
Clematis (*Clematis* spp.)
Climbing hydrangea (*Hydrangea petiolaris*)
Climbing roses (*Rosa* spp.)
Fiveleaf akebia (*Akebia quintata*)
Porcelain berry (*Ampelopsis brevipedunculata*)

▲ Clematis

ANNUALS AND TENDER PERENNIALS

Black-eyed Susan vine (*Thunbergia alata*)
Cup and saucer vine (*Cobaea scandens*)
Hyacinth bean (*Lablab purpureus*)
Morning glory (*Ipomoea* spp.)
Purple coral pea (*Hardenbergia violaceae*)
Sweet pea (*Lathyrus odoratus*)

▲ **Update an old stoop.** This house, once a white cottage with a shingle roof and small concrete stoop, was transformed with a coat of paint, metal roof, lush plantings, and a new stoop. This stoop is wider, built from stone and accented with eye-catching container plantings.

▲ **Small stoops can be artfully detailed.** This one features an interesting combination of cut stone and random stone—all placed in an octagonal arrangement.

Update an Old Stoop

For a front-yard facelift, consider sprucing up your existing stoop or steps. You can enlarge them, resurface them, add new railings or posts, and even change the portico design above them. Widening a small stoop to 6 by 9 feet or larger will give you extra space for a couple of containers, a small bench, and a few last words to guests. Resurfacing your stoop with thin flagstone, tile, or concrete pavers in a diagonal pattern will make your stoop look bigger even if it's not. And attaching planks of wood between the treads of open wooden stairs to create risers is a simple way to dress up a staircase. You'll enjoy the changes, and they'll add to the resale value of your home.

▲A broad stoop can double as a terrace so there's enough room for the entire family to sit out front on a nice evening. Here, the chair colors reflect house, shutter, and window-box colors to tie the space together.

Even if your entry is tiny, attention to details can make a big impression. And because you're working in a small space, you can put your money toward quality materials and craftsmanship rather than quantity. Consider upgrading your door hardware, buying a unique container for plantings, adding an antique light fixture, or resurfacing your landing and steps with thin stone, tile, or brick pavers. A small entry is the ideal spot for a patterned floor—whether treated concrete, a tile mosaic, or brick laid in a ruglike pattern. You can also add life to confined spaces by accenting the upright—vine-covered trellises, window boxes overflowing with trailing and erect flowers, planted baskets hanging from your portico, or clusters of containers with conical evergreens or tall topiaries.

Tiny Entry

Focus on details with a small entry.

Porches

The housing boom after World War II that resulted in oversimplified landscapes of little more than lawns and evergreen foundation plantings also contributed to the demise of front porches. Once common to architectural styles ranging from low-country cottages to grand Victorians to simple farmhouses, porches—like front-yard landscaping—are making a comeback. Not only do many new homes include a porch in the design, but homeowners are adding porches in record numbers to existing residences.

If you're adding on a porch, make sure it is at least 6 feet wide. Larger homes can easily support porches that are 8 or 10 feet wide. As with other outdoor structures, you'll need to check local building codes—especially those that apply to setbacks, the distance from the road that structures can be built.

▼Matching rail planters help unite this home's two porches. The lower porch also features container plantings and a place to sit. Shrubs hide the foundation but not the porch railing.

Porches come in many shapes and sizes. There are small corner porches, porches that run the length of the house front, and wraparound porches that surround the entire house. Many are screened—especially in mosquito-prone areas—and others are open. Porch railings run the gamut from wood to wrought iron, from simple wooden palings to elaborately turned and painted palings. Porches are the perfect spot for a bench, wicker chairs, porch swing, or set of rockers. If you have a large porch, you can even create a series of small outdoor living rooms.

Low plantings are often the most pleasing beneath porch railings, with taller plants at the house corners and on either side of the front steps. Fragrant, flowering vines can be trained up and across a porch—as long as you realize that the eave is likely to reduce the amount of sun and natural rainfall a vine receives. Choose from vines with greater shade tolerance, and consider adding supplemental irrigation for any plantings (vines or otherwise) beneath an eave. Pots of ferns, impatiens, and other shade-loving plants will love a porch setting. Porches are also perfect for hanging baskets or box planters (including the kind that hang on rails). For variety, try including small vines and trailing plants along with the annual flowers in your baskets. And if your hanging baskets are exposed to drying winds, make sure you choose large baskets that are better able to hold moisture.

Perennials frame this low porch, with towering hollyhocks anchoring the corners in summer.

Courtyards originated in warm-climate regions like southern California, the Southwest, and parts of the South settled by the Spanish, but they are becoming increasingly common throughout the country. They can be used to create outdoor living rooms screened from public view as well as from the environment. Walls, arbors, and plantings provide relief from the hot sun, wind, and noise (though rarely from rain, snow, or cold). These walls don't have to be high to offer a sense of enclosure; even low walls can create a cozy atmosphere.

▼A covered entry and attractive gate make a dramatic entrance to this New Orleans–style courtyard. A large pot filled with fragrant gardenias serves as a focal point as you enter. Inside are a water feature and several benches.

The principal reason for building a courtyard is to provide a protected area for enjoying the outdoors. Most often, that means a place to sit and talk, drink a cup of tea, or read the morning paper. But there are other uses too—dining, cooking, napping, entertaining, and even gardening. So when designing your courtyard, it helps to first think about how you'll use the space, and then allow enough room for those activities. While a chair or bench can be tucked into almost any nook or cranny, you'll need a minimum of 12 by 12 feet for a 4-foot table and chairs. A café table with two chairs will occupy about half that space.

You'll also need to think about wall height and how that affects your activities. High walls will create the greatest amount of privacy but will limit the amount of sunlight for gardening and can make a small courtyard feel claustrophobic. An arbor overhead will add immensely to the sense of enclosure in the courtyard but is best if it only covers part of it. Then you won't feel completely cut off from the sky, and it won't darken interior rooms too much.

Mocking Up a Courtyard

Try mocking up the layout of a courtyard, including the height of the walls, before finishing your plans. You can easily do this with some tall stakes placed at the corners, with string tied between them at the anticipated wall height. Then sit in a chair in this area to see how you feel. Leave it for a few days; notice the sun patterns and think about how they'll affect your activities. Imagine the views both in and out of the courtyard that you will be hiding or preserving. Move your wall stakes and change your string height to make any necessary adjustments before beginning construction.

◀**Though walls and fences** enclose most courtyards, hedges also work well. They just require frequent pruning to stay neat. This courtyard has a porous floor and doubles as a sunny garden spot. The owners enjoy sitting here in the evening, surrounded by fragrant roses and herbs.

▶**Masonry walls can be softened with plants, both inside and out.** Try espaliering a fruit tree, pyracantha, or pomegranate on a wide wall, and using climbing roses or other vines to scale tall walls or arbors.

▲**This fence-enclosed courtyard features** attractive flagstone paving and island beds for plantings. An arbor marks the entry and a pair of teak chairs offers a destination.

There are an infinite number of ways to define and enclose a courtyard. Your choice will be driven by your tastes, house style, budget, and time frame. The least expensive way to enclose an area is with a hedge, but even a fast-growing hedge can take several years to fill in. For more immediate results, you'll need to consider walls and fences. Those built from stone, brick, or wrought iron are the most expensive. Wooden fences and stuccoed concrete-block walls usually cost less and can be just as attractive in the right setting. Of course, not all your courtyard walls need to be the same. You might splurge on a stacked-stone wall near the front entry, with hedges or vine-covered fences along the sides.

To develop the gestalt of the various courtyard elements—the walls, ceiling (if any), flooring, and accents—the materials used need to complement rather than compete with each other. It's sort of a balancing act—providing contrast and interest without making the area too busy.

For flooring, a good rule of thumb is to make it interesting but not so busy that it calls attention to itself. An exception would be a courtyard where the flooring is the focal point—say, a pebble-mosaic "rug"—and the remainder of the courtyard is very simple. Most courtyards have masonry or gravel floors. Because courtyards are often shady areas and because they do not easily accommodate power equipment, a lawn is generally not a good choice—though there is no reason not to have a small patch of grass if you want.

▼**The courtyard of this postmodern home is** enclosed by the house and garage, as well as by a stucco fence, creating a private space for outdoor entertaining. An innovative water feature and plantings pay homage to the surrounding desert landscape. The principal colors of green, terra-cotta, and gray are echoed in the furniture, hardscape, containers, and plantings.

Buffering Neighborhood Noise

We learn about and respond to our environment by listening, as sounds trigger activity in our brains. Sounds can relax us, awaken us, or carry us to other places and times. By their constancy and rhythm, sounds can be comforting. Many natural sounds—the sighing of pines, rustling of leaves, gentle lulling of waves, or purring of a cat—trigger a soothing emotional response. On the other hand, many sounds of urban life are distracting: Consider screeching tires, honking horns, lawn mowers, and leaf blowers. Even the voices of people at the wrong time, place, or pitch can put us on edge.

That's why screening some sounds, while adding or attracting others, is so important where we live. We can include elements to create, encourage, ricochet, and amplify sounds. Sounds that put us on edge can be buffered with dense screening and camouflaged by introducing soothing, rhythmic sounds like the trickling of water or gentle ringing of chimes. Other random but natural sounds can be encouraged through interplay with the environment—whether it's rain falling on a tin roof, birds splashing in a fountain, or wind rustling among leaves.

▲A water feature placed near a front entry will help lower the blood pressure of arriving guests who have been battling traffic jams. In a courtyard, water draws your attention from distracting neighborhood noise so you can enjoy visiting with friends or reading a book.

Plants are always pleasing in a courtyard, as they soften all the hard surfaces, provide a touch of color, and add another layer of texture to the walls, floor, and canopy. Vines are especially welcome, as they can cling to walls, twine up posts and trellises, and dangle from overhead structures.

Ever since the paradise gardens of Persia, water has been appreciated in courtyards for its sound, beauty, and cooling effect. The walls of a courtyard will magnify the sound of falling water, and dappled light will reflect off it, enlivening the walls. A water feature in a courtyard simply cannot have its praises sung too highly.

A Japanese-Inspired Courtyard

The moment you peer through Stephen and Meg Carruthers's courtyard gate, you're hooked. It's not possible to pass this view without being lured in to sit a spell on the simply but sturdily crafted bench, to meditate as the fish swim in the nearby pond, or to study the intricate patterns of the flagstone path laid in puzzlelike fashion. Even the fence is intriguing—simple board slats arranged randomly on alternating sides of horizontal supports.

Courtyards are among the most intimate of entries, and this one is no exception.

▲ **The homeowner designed** this simply but sturdily built bench and placed it so one could sit and watch the fish in the pond.

◄ **Evergreens anchor this Japanese-style courtyard,** though it's not devoid of flowers. Architectural elements are designed from simple materials but used in interesting ways. A fish pond adds to the calming atmosphere.

◄The entry gate is inviting. With its clean, simple lines, it allows the view within to dominate.

Stephen, a professional landscaper, drew inspiration from Japanese gardens for this courtyard. The hardscaping is deliberate and restrained, with strong use of lines and natural materials like wood, flagstone, and boulders. Plantings are lush and green, with an emphasis on foliage and texture rather than flowers. Small sculptures placed with care throughout the courtyard further personalize the space. The result is a peaceful, inviting atmosphere—a perfect transitional space for welcoming guests to their home on the outskirts of Portland, Oregon.

The house provides two of the courtyard walls; the other two are made from naturally weathered board fences. Both walls and fences are softened with plantings—from heavenly bamboo near the front door to Japanese maples, bamboo, and an assortment of evergreens along the fence and an espaliered pomegranate against the house.

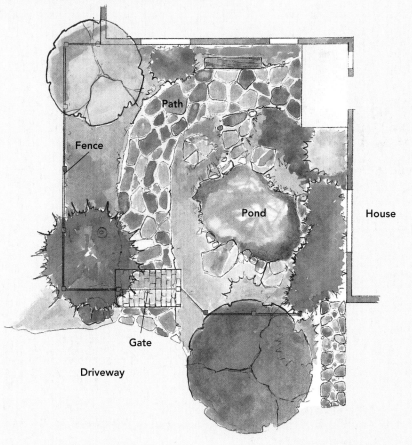

Path

Fence

Pond

House

Gate

Driveway

3

Paths and Steps

▶This brick path is laid in a herringbone pattern.

Well-designed paths do more than get you from one place to another. A neatly laid brick walk to the front door welcomes guests to the place you call "home." A curved stepping-stone path that vanishes behind a hedge creates a sense of intrigue. A short, straight path from the garage clearly signals the quickest route to the house. And a meandering, mulched path through a front-yard garden says it's time to slow down and smell the roses.

Though basically utilitarian, well-designed paths can create a special setting or mood. The length, direction, materials, and points of interest along the way all contribute to the experience of walking down a path. Even the simplest—a short, straight, concrete path— can be enhanced by laying a row of cobbles or bricks on either side, by resurfacing with mortared flagstone, thin bricks, or pavers, or by bordering it with plants that spill out onto its surface.

The relative formality or informality of a path is expressed in the way the path is laid out, the materials chosen, and how those materials are used. A straight brick path surrounded by a manicured lawn is decidedly more formal than a curving, dry-laid flagstone path softened with creeping plants, which is still not as informal as a mulched path edged in railroad timbers. Whether you

◀This gently curved path is dry-laid in a running-bond pattern. It leads through an inviting arbor from the driveway to the front door and doubles as edging between a perennial border and lawn.

◄An informal path simply doesn't get any more charming than this. Stepping-stones are softened and surrounded by blue star creeper, geraniums, and epimediums, causing you to slow down and watch your footfalls.

▼The flagstone used for this informal path closely matches the color of the painted brick. Tile, brick, and other materials used for paths can be color-coordinated with a house.

design a formal or informal path is often guided by the architecture of your home. Generally, the larger and more traditional the home, the more formal the paths.

When possible, match the colors and materials of paths to your house. This is one of the best ways to tie your landscape and architecture together. Most of the time, the choice of materials is obvious. For instance, a concrete path edged in brick would complement a brick home, and a flagstone path would look nice leading to a house with a stone foundation. If you have a new wood-frame house and are pouring a concrete path, consider seeding it with colored pebbles or adding stain to complement the color of your house paint. One of the best-looking designs I've seen was a quarry-tile and granite-cobble path leading to a light terra-cotta-colored house with clay roof tiles. The variable color of the roof tiles, which ran from deep terra-cotta to gray-purple, beautifully matched the tiles and granite.

▲A main path to a front door should be the widest path in the front landscape. Four feet is a good starting point, but don't be afraid to go wider. This path climbs a hill, so it includes steps with railings, landings, and even a bench along the way. Note how the paving patterns change to differentiate the steps from the landings.

A well-laid front path clearly leads visitors to the main entrance of your home. It's like a red carpet rolled out to greet friends and family. As such, it should be your most formal path in the landscape, with the smoothest surface.

The main path to your front door should also be the widest path in your yard. A wide path, by its very nature, commands attention. You should follow it without hesitation. It's nice to make this path generous enough for two people to walk side by side. Four feet is a good width for most yards; wider paths may be best for a larger house or where plants spill onto the path. Occasionally, the front door is hidden or may not be the preferred entrance to a home. A wide path will lead visitors to your entry, no matter where the door.

One of the first issues you'll need to address is how visitors will reach your front entry. Will you speed them along, or give them reason to pause? The most basic path is a straight one that leads directly to the door. In fact, a straight path will

An Enchanting Entry

▲ **Originally a 14-step climb,** this front entry is now approached along a zigzagging path with short intermediate risers.

When Mahan Rykiel Associates was hired to renovate this residential landscape just outside the Baltimore city limits, among their first challenges was a front entry with a 14-riser stairway and a 7-foot drop in elevation between the front door and the driveway. Their solution was to spread the steps out by creating a series of garden terraces with paths running their length.

Near the driveway, matching stacked-stone piers and an allée of cherry trees—a sight to behold in early spring and inviting any time of year—mark the path's entrance. As you make your way along the bluestone path to the next terrace, you are greeted by three charming bronze piglets and you discover a tiny rectangular lawn surrounded by attractive plantings. And finally, as you approach the front entry, you are invited to relax on a generous flagstone terrace that offers seating for four and a lovely view of rolling hills and flowering dogwoods.

This path winds through rather than alongside plantings, and at each grade change, it jogs in a different direction through different scenery. As a result, it makes you want to slow down, breathe more deeply, and inhale the fragrance of freshly mown grass wafting from a nearby field.

◄ **The path takes several distinct jogs** that change the scenery en route to the front door.

▼ **The lowest section of** the path travels through an allée of cherry trees that flower in early spring and form a graceful canopy in any season.

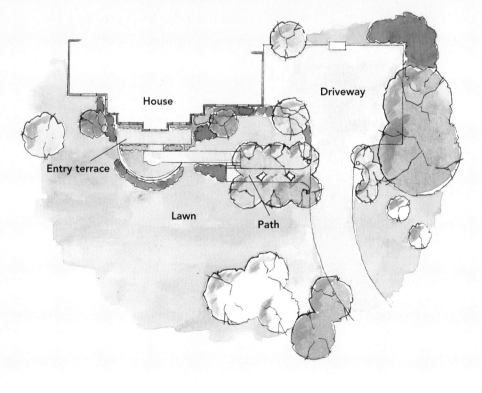

House

Driveway

Entry terrace

Lawn

Path

cause your eyes to immediately rest on the door, making you feel as if you have arrived even before you walk a few feet down that path. A straight path marks the shortest distance between two points, so it's the easiest and least expensive path to build. If you live in a snowy climate, that means less snow to shovel. A curving path, however, is enchanting. It is pleasing to look at and encourages one to slow down and enjoy the experience of walking down that path. Zigzagging paths have a similar effect and add interest to your landscape.

It's helpful to lay a garden hose (warmed by the sun so it bends easily) or planks of wood along the proposed route of a path. See how it looks up close and from a distance. Walk along the path to see how it feels. You'll know immediately if you've placed it too close to a prickly holly, headed it in the direction of an undesirable view, or sited it on uneven ground. You will also be able to tell whether the width is comfortable or feels a little crowded. Play with the layout: Change the width, flare the path at one or both ends, make the curves gentler or deeper, shift it either direction by a foot or two, or try an altogether different layout.

As you contemplate the layout of your path, think about its point of origination. Though that may seem obvious, paths are often misplaced. The guiding question is: Where do guests park? Or if you come and go regularly from the front door as well, where do you park? If there is ample parking in the driveway, there may be no need to run a path to the street. If you have little or no driveway parking, a path from the street may be sufficient. Often, two paths make the most sense—one from the sidewalk and a second from the driveway. Another option is to run a small path alongside the driveway to the street. This is a nice option if your driveway handles most of your parking needs but leaves little room for walking once it is filled with cars.

▲ **Curving paths are often more interesting** than straight ones. They force you to slow down and enjoy the journey. This one originates in the driveway where visitors park.

Materials
for Main Paths

Bricks are very durable. They range in color from sandy yellow to brown to deep red. The glazing process can render the finish either dull or slightly glossy, and bricks are sold in many textures, including smooth, stippled, and matte. They also vary in thickness: Common bricks used for paths are about twice the thickness of facing bricks for a wall or fireplace. You can also buy old or used bricks; just keep in mind that they are often porous and subject to spalling in cold, wet climates. They can also be odd sized.

Stone is also durable and immediately gives an established look to the landscape. One of the best choices for walkways is flagstone—a flat, hard, and irregularly shaped but evenly layered stone that is split into slabs. Bluestone, slate, sandstone, and water-washed sandstone are all flagstones. Because of its irregular shape, laying flagstone is like piecing together a puzzle. It's not difficult but can be time consuming.

▲**Random flagstone is usually mortared for front paths** to keep it from shifting underfoot.

Many of these stones are also sold as cut pavers—which come as square or rectangular pieces of even thickness that can be fit together quickly. They are commonly used in formal settings. Flagstones, whether irregular or cut, can be either dry-laid or mortared.

Concrete pavers are versatile, attractive, and durable and can be laid in a multitude of patterns. Less expensive than stone or brick, they come in an assortment of shapes, sizes, and colors. Concrete pavers do not require mortar, are three times stronger than poured concrete, and shift without breaking as soil conditions change—making them ideal for cold climates.

Poured concrete has a new look. It can be pigmented, stained, texturized, scored, or combined with aggregate to create an attractive, durable surface. It's much easier to treat concrete at installation than it is to refinish existing concrete—though there are companies that have developed techniques for that too. To update an existing concrete path, it may be easier to widen it with a band of bricks or cobbles, or to mortar thin pavers or flagstone over the concrete base.

▲**Concrete is the most affordable paving material. It can** be dressed up with bands of brick or cobbles as well as pigmented, stained, texturized, or seeded with aggregate.

▲ In wet climates, you need paths with good traction. This Pacific Northwest garden features a coarse concrete path edged and banded with brick. It is both attractive and safe.

As well as being obvious in direction, a main path should provide secure footing in any weather. Loose materials, such as stepping-stones, chipped gravel, or mulch, are best reserved for secondary paths. Instead, select materials that provide a consistent surface and lay them so that they cannot shift underfoot. That's why poured-concrete and mortared-stone, -brick, and -tile paths are such good choices when they lead to a front door.

How the weather affects the surface of the materials should also be considered. Slate can be slippery in rainy weather, brick can become mossy in damp shade, and non-mortared surfaces are tough to shovel after a snowstorm. Flagstone with a slightly textured surface will be less slippery; concrete simply edged with brick may be a better choice for damp shade; and smooth, mortared surfaces make more sense in snow country.

Create Pattern with Brick

One of the greatest benefits of using brick is its ability to create a pattern in your walk. There are many classic brick patterns: Running bond, herringbone, stack bond, and basketweave are just a few. Bricks can be laid as straight or gently curving paths, or even in a concentric circle as the focal point of a path. As a rule of thumb, a pattern that runs with the path (such as running bond) will move your eye quickly down a path. A pattern that crosses the width of the path (such as basketweave) will slow down eye movement. On long paths, try breaking up patterns into sections or panels with periodic header courses (bands of brick

Brick Patterns

Basketweave

Herringbone

Running bond

Stack bond

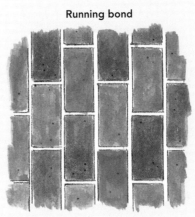

across a path) or combining patterns for a more interesting pathway. You can also combine brick with stone or concrete for added visual texture, vary the hue in bricks, or replace some bricks with 8-inch-square tiles for an artistic touch.

Most bricks are 4 inches wide and 8 inches long, but they do come in different sizes. An odd-sized brick will throw off a pattern, so be sure to lay out a few sections of your pattern at the brickyard before placing your order.

◀ **Existing concrete paths and steps can often** be overlaid with brick or other pavers. However, you need to be careful where the path meets the driveway. A slight grade change can easily cause someone to trip. Here, the owners solved that problem by cutting the transitional bricks at a slope.

Secondary Paths

Beyond the main path to the door, you may find it helpful to create one or more secondary paths that lead to the side yard, a seating area, the garage, a flower garden, or even the neighbor's yard. Such secondary paths should be less formal in style and slightly narrower—3 feet is ideal for frequently traveled paths, but as little as 1½ feet may do in other areas.

Another factor that influences a path's size and style is its relationship to the house and surrounding landscape. The farther from the house, the narrower and more informal paths tend to become. Of course, in all but the most casual of situations, it is still best to choose and place materials so people walking on the path don't have to pick their way carefully along.

▲ **Secondary paths need not** connect to a main path. In this case, a stepping-stone path runs from the front lawn through a narrow side yard. Though the stepping-stone path is much narrower, the materials complement those in the main path.

◀ **Distinguish between primary and secondary paths.** The widest, smoothest path should lead to the front door. Narrower, less formal paths can lead to other parts of the yard or garden. Here, the owner differentiated paths in both size and materials.

► A breezeway runs from the separate garage to the kitchen, offering protection in wet weather. A short path also connects the driveway to the breezeway—creating an attractive secondary entry for family and close friends.

▼ Recycle materials. This homeowner took out a concrete path that once led to the front door but recycled the broken concrete by mixing it creatively with bricks and a few river cobbles for a side-yard path.

I often match the materials to the main path but use them in a more casual way. For instance, if a main path is laid in mortared brick, a narrower secondary path in dry-laid brick would lend continuity to the landscape without drawing attention from the main path. Stepping-stone paths complement wider, mortared-stone paths in a similar way. If using stepping-stones, choose those with the smoothest surface possible and anchor them securely. The top of the stones should be flush with the ground.

Another option is to use different materials for secondary paths. Chipped gravel and granite fines are excellent choices, and mulched paths are ideal winding through a front-yard garden.

Materials for Secondary Paths

Chipped gravel is small, irregular stone that comes in an assortment of colors and crunches softly beneath your feet. It kicks up easily and is difficult to shovel after a snowstorm, but it drains quickly after a rain and is an excellent choice for informal paths. You'll need something to keep it in bounds; cobbles or some sort of wood or metal edging will do the trick.

Quarry fines have a finely crushed, irregular texture and come in both gray and a pleasant ochre-brown. A quarry-fine path is attractive, affordable, and easily maintained. Edging will keep it neat, or you can allow it to blend in more naturally with plants as a garden path.

Stepping-stones are generally flagstones or flat fieldstones secured at ground level with grass, herbs, or other creeping plants between them. Decorative stepping-stones made from concrete are also available, or you can make your own—perhaps with an imbedded tile, glass, or pebble mosaic.

Cobbles come in two varieties: cut-granite cobbles and rounded river cobbles. Because they form an uneven surface when laid, cobbles should be kept to secondary paths except when used as edging. Cut-granite cobbles may be dry-laid or mortared and are easier to walk on than river cobbles, which must be mortared for stability and are generally reserved for creative applications.

Mulch is the most casual and least expensive path material to install. It looks lovely winding through the woods or a garden. Edging can help keep it in place, though it's generally not a necessity. You must replenish a mulch path every year or so, but it nourishes the soil as it breaks down.

◀ Secondary paths are generally less structured than main paths. They can be narrower, less formal, and created from a broader range of materials. This quarry-fine path meanders through a naturalistic front-yard garden.

▲ Stepping-stones are an excellent choice for providing access to the water spigot or other utility area. Choose from flat stones, bricks, and concrete stepping-stones, or make your own. These feature pebble mosaics set in concrete rounds.

Sidewalks

Sidewalks come in two basic variations—those placed directly at the curb and those with a small strip of ground between the sidewalk and street. The first is more common in commercial districts, the second in residential areas—though it varies from one town or neighborhood to the next. My favorites are those with a strip of earth because they can be landscaped.

Most sidewalk strips are devoid of everything except grass, fire hydrants, and maybe a few street trees. But just think what a nicely planted sidewalk strip would do for your evening walks around the neighborhood, not to mention the setting for your house. By creating a small garden area on either side of the sidewalk (in the strip and in your yard), you actually make a small public garden that your neighbors can also enjoy. Use only the toughest plants—those that can handle the heat, dryness, piles of plowed snow, plants, and occasional footsteps—and avoid plants that will soon outgrow their allotted space or snag the cloth-

▼**Think beyond the straight and narrow.** This sidewalk landing flows like a river.

Paths Lead the Way

Not all house sites are flat, and not all front entries face the street. Take this contemporary home in the hills of northern California. Built on a steep curve, it can be accessed from the street in two locations—at house level by way of a short driveway, or from 15 feet below, near a detached garage. Both entries were designed for vehicular use, and neither approached the front door.

When Brad and Nancy Lewis hired the landscape firm of Four Dimensions, circulation was a top priority. The straight wooden staircase from the garage to the front door was beginning to decay, and the owners had to give detailed instructions on the phone to first-time visitors for how to

▲ **From the upper drive, the wider, mortared path** clearly leads to the front door, while the narrower, stepping-stone path leads to the kitchen door. A small cairn marks the diverging paths.

◀The main entry is actually from below. These meandering stone steps replaced a straight wooden staircase. Landings ease the climb, while plantings and a water feature make it more enjoyable.

▶These curved steps make an attractive entry and match the stone paths. A bench serves as both a focal point and place to relax. The covered entry provides space for packages and cover in inclement weather.

reach the house. Four Dimensions started by replacing the staircase with a meandering curve of stone steps. The curve allowed the designers to break up the climb into a series of shorter flights with landings. This lessened the apparent steepness and made the passage more comfortable and inviting. Plantings, stacked-stone walls, and water features made it more interesting. Near the bottom of the steps, a new street entry was created and marked with a boulder and house numbers to encourage visitors to walk up the steps through the garden.

On the upper level, which is still used by the family and some guests, are two paths—the wider, mortared path is clearly the main path, and it leads to the front entry. A smaller stepping-stone path veers toward the kitchen door. A stone cairn marks the fork in the paths.

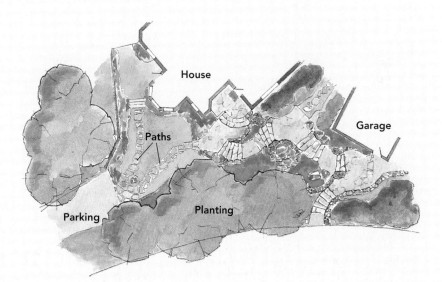

House

Garage

Paths

Parking

Planting

◄ **Coordinate colors and** materials carefully. The flagstone in this main path echoes the warm tones of the stucco in the house and matching walls near the street.

ing of those who park next to them. Plantings can run the gamut from evergreen ground covers to long-blooming perennials to mixed plantings with seasonal interest.

When you landscape your sidewalk strip, be sure to leave several landing areas for getting in and out of the car. Paving materials of some sort work best, as they'll keep your shoes dry in wet weather. Brick, flagstone, and pea gravel work equally well, so choose a surface that complements your other landscaping materials. If your main path runs from the house to the sidewalk, consider continuing it between the sidewalk and street by matching the width, materials, and any patterns. These landings should be at least 3 feet wide.

Though not all streets have sidewalks, just about any house can. If you have lawn that runs to the curb, consider adding a narrow sidewalk if your guests frequently park along the street. Then they won't step out of the car onto wet grass.

▲ **Don't have a sidewalk? Add one. Guests** will appreciate stepping out onto a solid surface rather than into the grass or other plantings. This one also presents a trim appearance where the yard meets the street.

Steps and Handicap Ramps

▲ **If you need to add steps to your path** for a grade change, try to avoid a single step. Two steps (counting the grade level, as shown here) are much easier to see. Changing the pattern at steps helps too. This cut-bluestone path features bull-nosed edges.

Unless your property is flat, you'll need to decide whether a gently sloped path or steps provide the safest passage. The guiding rule for deciding this is to consider the degree of the slope. If you have a 6 percent or less change in grade (which can be measured as a 3-inch drop over a 4-foot run), you're probably better off with a gentle slope, which is much easier to negotiate, easier to install, and less surprising than a single step. Just be sure to avoid paving materials that will dislodge easily or become slippery when wet, and make sure your slope tapers gradually and evenly. If the grade change is greater than 6 percent, you'll need to install steps.

Where there is a steep grade change, steps and surrounding retaining walls are major architectural features that should be carefully designed. The expertise of a landscape architect would be very helpful in this situation. As a general guideline, avoid long runs of steps. Try not to design more than eight steps without a landing, though in some cases this is difficult because the grade change is so great. At a landing, you can change the direction of the steps—veering slightly right or left—adding interest to the landscape and breaking up the climb. Provide a low wall or bench as a resting spot along the way.

If you're designing or installing your own steps, keep safety in mind. Your goal is to create a rise-to-run ratio in which most people would take a natural stride. Good combinations include a 5½-inch rise with a 15-inch tread, a 6½-inch rise with a 14-inch tread, and a 4½-inch rise with a 17-inch tread. Keep it consistent throughout and light the

◄Steps need not be straight. These broad steps are laid in an elegant curve, issuing an invitation to come see what lies beyond. The concrete is softened by plantings that gently spill over the edges without becoming a tripping hazard.

steps so they can be seen in the dark. With three or more steps, put in a handrail. If possible, highlight the beginning of a run of steps with a different paving material or pattern to call attention to the grade change. For instance, you might add a row of bricks to the edge of concrete steps. On brick steps, you might vary the brick color or turn the bricks a different direction along the edge. Boulders placed beside steps are also a good way to emphasize the grade change.

Concrete, flagstone, and brick are all excellent materials for steps. Aggregate can be added to concrete to create greater surface friction. And a slightly porous or textured flagstone, versus a solid, smooth-surfaced stone, will provide better traction in wet weather. In an informal setting, railroad ties can be used, but they will require ongoing maintenance to keep the fill behind them level for a safe climbing surface. As a general rule, railroad ties are best reserved for steps along secondary paths.

▲A wrought-iron handrail was artfully crafted and attached to this wall for safety and support. Such unexpected details add a nice finishing touch to the landscape.

►**Mixed materials create a** pleasing contrast; here, that contrast calls attention to the steps, which improves safety. These poured-concrete steps are offset by boulders and patterned brick.

▼**This handicap ramp was** designed both to be safe and to blend in with the house. It provides easy access to a charming cottage garden as well as the driveway.

Ease of accessibility to your home is a key consideration if a family member or frequent visitor uses a wheelchair or has difficulty negotiating steps. Most states have developed useful guidelines for providing access for disabled persons. These guidelines cover slope, length of run, ramp configuration, handrails, landings, and other features.

Wood is the most commonly used material for building ramps. It is affordable, versatile, and easy to build with. If you live in a brick or mortared home, a concrete ramp faced with brick or stone will blend more seamlessly with the architecture. Railings for ramps can be designed to match the house as well. Landscape a ramp much as you would a small porch or stoop, bringing plantings up to the edge without interfering with the use of the rails. A mix of evergreen and deciduous plants will screen the foundation and provide seasonal interest. And finally, a few fragrant plants placed at nose level will be much appreciated.

Driveways and Parking

4

▶**This simple, winding drive** is laid in local crushed shells rather than gravel.

As children, we view driveways as playgrounds—places for riding bikes, playing hopscotch, or shooting hoops. As adults, we view them a little differently. Driveways provide access to our house, give us a place to park our cars, and offer a smooth surface for rolling out the garbage and recyclables each week for pickup. Sometimes we hold yard sales there, wash the car, or even garden— either in containers or alongside the drive.

Though primarily utilitarian, new driveways and parking areas should be designed to complement your home and landscape. At a minimum, driveways shouldn't detract— though this can be a challenge considering the amount of space they often take up. Driveways can require a substantial outlay of cash, so it pays to think them through carefully before the bulldozer arrives. If you live in a house with a less than desirable driveway, there's no reason to lose hope. There are a number of ways to update a driveway without having to start from scratch.

The size and shape of a lot, its grade, the location of the house and garage entrances, additional parking needs, and the amount of street traffic all impact the design of a driveway. As you make plans to design a new driveway or update

◀**This brick driveway marks the beginning of a gracious entry. A low stone pillar topped with** a planted urn creates a sort of gateway.

an existing one, you'll need to ask yourself the following
questions:

- **Ingress and egress**—Is it safe to back out of your driveway or should you only drive forward onto the street? Can
  you see oncoming traffic?
- **Ease of access**—Do you have room to maneuver the car,
  open your doors, and get things in and out comfortably?
  Is the grade change too abrupt or a curve too tight? If your
  house is set back from the road, is there room for a fire
  truck in an emergency, or for delivery trucks to turn
  around without gouging your lawn?
- **Parking**—How many cars do you need to accommodate?
  Do you have adequate space for them or do you need
  more parking? Where might you place additional parking
  so that it can be somewhat screened from view?
- **Grade changes**—Does your driveway have a flat or gentle
  grade, or is it so steep that you can't see to back up and
  have difficulty getting in and out of the car? Would a

▲ **Median strips in a driveway,**
whether the drive is paved or
gravel, can be planted with
low-growing herbs and wildflowers to create a colorful,
low-maintenance carpet. In
this case, the median strip
complements the native
desert wildflowers in the front-
yard garden.

longer, winding drive better suit your lot than a shorter, straight one? Does your car scrape anywhere along the drive, such as at the street or garage entry?

- **Drainage**—Where will the runoff from your driveway go? Do you have low points where you slosh through puddles after a rainstorm?

- **Function**—Will you use your driveway for activities besides parking, ingress, and egress? Does it currently double as a pathway for visitors parked on the road? Do children play there? Can it double as an area for entertainment? Would a smooth, natural, or decorative surface best suit these activities?

- **Aesthetics**—Would you like to de-emphasize your driveway or break it up visually? Are there certain areas such as the street entry, a parking court, or a half circle near your front door that you want to accent?

▼Because the driveway and parking area fall between the garage and front entry, this area was designed to double as a courtyard. It includes a bench and container plantings along the periphery, as well as an attractive stone wall surrounded by plantings.

Storm Spurs Landscape Makeover

When Hurricane Opal struck Atlanta in 1995, it toppled more than 5,000 of the city's largest oaks. One of those was in Arabelle and Grant Luckhardt's front yard. It knocked out the power and blocked traffic for a full week, and left their shady front-yard plantings exposed to full sun. But the Luckhardts turned this event into a good excuse for a complete landscape makeover and called in landscape designer Paula Refi for the job.

Arabelle loved gardens, and that's what she wanted to see when she looked out all her windows. As she says, "I wanted the

▲**After the storm,** an uprooted tree and other plantings were removed. This shot was taken before the new, wider driveway had been paved, the additional parking space had been added, and the front-yard garden had been planted.

◀**This front garden looks as good from the** street as it does from the living room window. Shrubs loosely enclose a small lawn and serve as a backdrop for perennials, annuals, and bulbs.

►**During the landscape renovation,** the driveway was widened and repaved. A parallel parking slot was created when a section of sloped lawn was cut out and replaced with an attractive stone wall.

front garden to be directed as much at me in the house as at the public." So Paula enclosed the front yard with a mix of small ornamental trees and shrubs and then planted both the inside and street side with perennials and bulbs. Window boxes were also added to bring flowers within even closer view. A small patch of lawn remains in the center of the yard.

Of course, this makeover entailed more than transforming the front yard into a garden. The slope next to the driveway was replaced with a stacked-stone retaining wall, and the old driveway was replaced with a new, wider one. In addition, a pull-in parking slot was added between the driveway and stone wall for the large van Arabelle was driving at the time. Says Arabelle, who has since retired the van to plantmobile status, "This was one of the best decisions we made. Having a dry-stacked wall gave a finished look to the front yard, and that parking space made it so much easier to load and unload the van." Originally, the stone wall was planted with sun-loving creeping perennials, but things continue to change in this garden— as the new trees are now creating shade of their own.

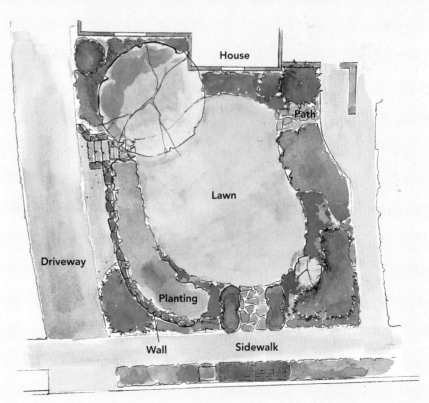

Driveways

Not only do we have more cars per household than ever before, but the average car is bigger than before. Just look at the number of luxury cars, trucks, and sport-utility vehicles on any highway. That's why most new driveways are 11 or 12 feet wide for a single-car garage and 20 feet wide for a two-car garage. Older driveways, which accommodated smaller cars, were often only 8 or 9 feet wide. Though cars can still be driven on them, they are more difficult to maneuver, and when you step out of these cars, you often find yourself standing on the lawn. As a result, some homeowners are ripping out and replacing old driveways, while others are widening existing drives by edging them with bricks, pavers, cut cobbles, and stone.

The simplest driveway, both to install and maneuver, is a straight one with plenty of clearance from walls, steep

▲ **Attractively detailed valances placed over garage doors** give vines a place to grow and soften the doors' visual impact.

▲This short driveway makes the most of materials, but in an uncommon way—by including both whole and broken bricks. The result is both attractive and functional.

◀Stones, pavers, or cut cobbles can also be placed in the center of a drive, replacing the old-fashioned grassy median strip. The materials require no upkeep but break up the pavement in a similar way.

shoulders, and plantings. Though it's easy to pull into a straight driveway, backing out can be difficult if you live on a busy road or have limited visibility. Flaring the drive at the street will give you more room to turn, and adding a turnaround slot will eliminate the need to back out into the street. In a pinch, the turnaround can also serve as an additional parking space.

Straight driveways, when they lead to a garage, pose a unique landscaping challenge: They lead your eyes (as well as your car) straight to the garage door. What you really want to call attention to is your home and the landscaping. There are several good ways to deal with this. First, create pattern in the driveway with bands of bricks, stones, or pavers that span the width of the drive. This will slow your eye down, and even lead it to the edges of the drive where you may have nice plantings or paths. Cluster large container plantings on either side of the garage door or build an arbor for vines above it to draw your immediate attention to something besides the door. And if your garage door is plain or worn, you might consider investing in a new door with windows or nice detailing. Don't go overboard, though—too much detailing will draw attention from the rest of the house.

Where space permits, a curving driveway is often more interesting. If laid out in a pleasing way, it will emphasize your house and landscape rather than your garage, carport, or parking area. If your lot slopes as well, you can decrease

Asphalt versus Concrete

Asphalt and concrete are the two most common materials for driveways in America. Asphalt is better suited to cold climates, concrete to hot climates. Either works well in moderate climates.

Asphalt is produced from petroleum and mixed with small stone particles. It is delivered hot to the site, dumped into a paving machine, spread in layers 4 to 8 inches deep, and then compacted with a heavy roller to create a smooth, firm, black surface. Both affordable and durable, it should last for many years. Asphalt is a good choice for cold climates, as it will withstand wide fluctuations in temperature and is especially resilient in extreme cold. Also, because it is black, it readily absorbs heat to help melt snow and ice. It is less suitable for areas of extreme heat because it softens and can easily be rutted or gouged. Asphalt drives will also dissolve or develop permanent soft spots if subjected to oil and gas spills. The look of asphalt can be improved by covering the surface with pea gravel in a layer of emulsion to help it blend in better with the surrounding landscape and to give it a longer-lasting finish.

Poured concrete is the best paving for driveways in warmer zones. It is slightly more expensive than asphalt, but is longer lasting if installed properly and can stand extreme heat. In cold climates, concrete is susceptible to cracking and spalling in winter's freeze-and-thaw cycles. Concrete has taken on a new look in recent years. It can be pigmented, stained with chemicals, topped with exposed aggregate, etched with acid, scored, pocked with salt, stamped, sandblasted, or coated with acrylic. It can be made to resemble bricks, stones, or pavers, or it can be combined with bricks, stones, or pavers to emphasize a street entrance or parking court. Used as edging or bands, it can accent and visually break up a large expanse of paving.

▲**Concrete can be stamped to look more like brick**—a nice detail at the street entry.

▲ **Curving driveways should be generous** in width for easy maneuvering. This one has a well-defined raised edge surrounded by mixed plantings.

the gradient by lengthening and curving your driveway. For safety, comfort, and driving ease, driveways shouldn't have more than a 12 percent grade (rise or fall of more than 12 feet in 100). On curves, a lower grade is preferred so cars will have good traction in wet weather. Where a slope meets a flat area, decrease the grade so vehicles do not scrape. At the street, the grade should be no more than 6 percent; where it meets a garage, it should be held to 4 percent.

When designing curving driveways, consider both the approach to the house and the views along the way. Walk the proposed course, and note anything that should be highlighted or screened. The curves of a driveway should have a minimum centerline radius of 20 feet. And where fire trucks would have to use the driveway to reach the house, curves should have a minimum centerline radius of at least 50 feet.

If you have a level front yard with a depth of at least 30 feet and a width of at least 70 feet, a half-circle drive might be a good choice. The major advantage of a half-circle driveway is that it has both an entrance and an exit, so you never have to back out into traffic. Also, half-circle drives usually come quite close to the front door, convenient during stormy weather or for guests arriving for a party, and easier for people with limited mobility. And visually, an arcing driveway places the focus on the house instead of the garage. Since half-circle drives can be coupled with straight drives that run to a garage or parking area, adding a half circle is a good way to update an existing drive. You can also detail the half circle, or at least the section near the front door, with an alternate paving material or edging to help focus attention on your front entry. However, half circles tend to divide your front yard visually, and adding more paving materials creates more runoff for storm drains.

In larger front yards with a depth of 90 feet or more, you might consider making a full circle or looped driveway. Circles generally look best with formal or symmetrically designed homes, while loops are appropriate for informal settings. Circular and looped driveways can also have spurs for garage access or additional parking.

▲ **A modified half-circle with a twist.** This one is edged and banded to better integrate with the path to the front door. Guests park along this half-circle drive; access to the garage is through the far driveway spur.

Circle Drives

Half-circle driveway

Loop driveway

Parking Bays, Pull-Offs, and Parking Courts

As a society, we've come to rely upon cars. We can't do the shopping, get to work, or take the kids to school without them. Households with three or more vehicles are common, yet few houses have garages to accommodate them all. Making matters worse, garages are often used as storage or work areas, which sometimes takes precedence over parking. As a result, our streets and driveways have become clogged with vehicles.

The simplest solution for increasing parking is adding a parking bay alongside a driveway. It can be placed either parallel or perpendicular to a driveway, or can be angled for

▼A pea-gravel pad creates additional parking without being obtrusive and allows water to drain freely into the soil beneath.

◄No garage, but plenty of parking. This two-car slot, carved out of a front corner of the lot, takes up little space but gets the cars off the street. Because it was put on a lot with a sloped front yard, retaining walls and steps were added. The retaining wall also enabled the owners to create a level lawn.

several cars—much like what you might see in a parking lot (only without the painted stripes). Placed near a garage, a perpendicular parking bay can double as a turnaround space for cars backing out of the garage. In this case, the closest edge of the turnaround should be at least 22 feet from the face of the garage, with a turning radius of 10 feet. A single space should be approximately 20 feet long and 12 feet wide; a double space should be 22 feet wide. For a parallel parking bay, allow plenty of room to maneuver—about 25 feet long next to the driveway, tapering to 18 feet on the outside.

The constraints of a small yard challenge even the best designers when parking must be integrated in a plan. Even so, I've seen some wonderful solutions. When there's not room for a driveway, there is often enough space to pave a single or double parking space, or pull-off, along the sidewalk or street. Just be sure to check your local codes first and obtain appropriate permits for cutting any curbs. Since this kind of off-street parking is very public, pay attention to design details and consider adding a low fence, wall, or hedge for screening (provided it doesn't block your view when backing out). If there really isn't room for off-street

Adding a Parking Space

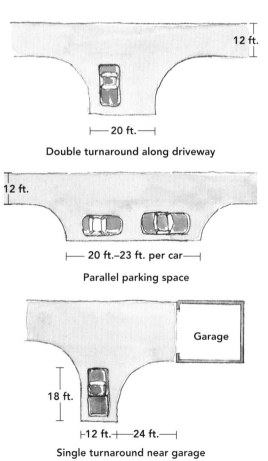

12 ft.

20 ft.

Double turnaround along driveway

12 ft.

20 ft.–23 ft. per car

Parallel parking space

Garage

18 ft.

12 ft. 24 ft.

Single turnaround near garage

Permeable Paving Surfaces

Permeable paving surfaces allow rainwater to seep back into the earth rather than run off into storm drains. This is especially important along driveways, because the oil, gas, and antifreeze that leak from cars are a significant source of water pollution. With a permeable surface, the soil acts as a filter, absorbing pollutants before the water percolates into the water table.

Gravel driveways are a natural choice for rural environments. Crushed gravel comes in several grades, or sizes, and varies slightly in color from one region to another. It is the most economical of all driveways to install, but new gravel must be spread regularly, and keeping weeds to a minimum can sometimes be a challenge. Though gravel is ideal for level lots, it's not a good choice where the grade exceeds 8 percent.

Pea gravel creates a beautiful surface that blends well into the surrounding landscape. Small stone that comes in a range of muted colors, it crunches subtly beneath car tires to announce the arrival of guests. That beauty comes at a higher cost, though. Pea gravel

▲This pull-off doubles as a parking space and turnaround. It is edged in cut cobbles, paved in gravel, and somewhat screened from the house by a low hedge.

▲Open-celled pavers can be planted with grass to create a permeable, environmentally friendly surface.

must be replaced often, and recent studies show that the regular removal of gravel from rivers is detrimental to the environment.

Open-cell pavers are grids of high-density plastic or concrete set on a prepared base, filled with soil, and planted with a sturdy turf grass that can handle cars. Once the grass becomes established, the pavers blend almost seamlessly into the surrounding landscape, especially if that landscape features any lawn. Open-cell pavers provide a firm, level surface that won't settle into ruts. However, the turf grass requires water, fertilization, and routine care.

Pervious concrete and asphalt are fairly new to the scene but have tremendous potential for reducing excessive runoff. They offer a smooth, sturdy surface like traditional concrete and asphalt, but allow water to seep through to a crushed gravel base that acts as a water reservoir. These materials are stable on flat ground but are generally not recommended for steep grades.

▲ **Details transform a parking area into a parking court.** Here, a millstone, cut cobbles, and stacked-stone retaining wall enhance a utilitarian space.

▶ **This large parking area** was transformed into a parking court with inset stones and soft screening provided by low shrubs and arbors.

parking, at least make sure that on-street parking has a clear, level landing area. Sections of brick or stone make a welcoming pad for passengers getting out of their car.

It's important to integrate the parking into the landscape. For visual interest and to reduce the apparent size of a driveway, consider paving parking areas with materials different from those used on the driveway. Pea gravel and open-cell pavers planted with grass will help parking areas blend into the landscape; patterned paving will emphasize the landscape. Either approach can work as long as it harmonizes with the house and landscape.

While a slab of concrete or a few yards of gravel make a functional parking space, attention to detail can transform that same space into a parking court. Parking courts, be-

Brick, Stone, and Pavers

Bricks, stones, and concrete pavers are classic paving materials that come in a wide range of colors, shapes, sizes, and textures. Styles are available to complement any house, and they can be dry-laid or mortared in an almost infinite range of patterns. Since they all require much hand labor, they are more costly than other driveway paving materials. But considering how long they last, and how much they add to the landscape, solid pavers are often worth the expense.

To give your driveway a pleasing look without breaking the bank, use bands or patterns of these higher-cost materials as accents in a base of treated concrete. Add a section of pavers at the street entry or near the front door of a half-circle driveway, or use them to create additional parking areas.

▲ **Older driveways can be easily widened** by adding cut cobbles, bricks, pavers, or even stone turned on edge.

cause they are carefully designed and landscaped, have more flexibility in terms of their placement. A parking court can be placed either right at the house on a smaller or urban lot, or away from the house on a larger property. It should accommodate at least two cars with ample room for opening and closing doors—at least 24 feet wide by 19 feet deep.

By surrounding parking courts with freestanding or retaining walls, you can transform them into courtyard-like settings. They may also be accented with clipped evergreen hedges, container plantings, large urns, garden statuary, columns, arbors, or water features. Two or three different paving materials are typically used, and patterns are often set into the central area of the parking court. Millstones, if you can find them, also make an interesting centerpiece for a parking court.

Parking Does Double Duty

Landscape architect Warren Simmonds made use of every square inch in this 25- by 35-foot space in Mill Valley, California. There's parking for one car, a tiny lawn, a patio for entertaining, and a small garden. To get that much into a lot this size required some creative thinking.

A swinging gate would have taken up nearly a quarter of the front yard. But by using a gate that rolls into a fence pocket, he was able to place the parking space closer to the street and add a patio next to the house. A small boxwood hedge provides screening between the patio and

▲**A small nook serves as a patio** with seating for five. Plantings and a wall (which can be seen in the other photos) provide plenty of privacy, despite the close proximity of neighbors.

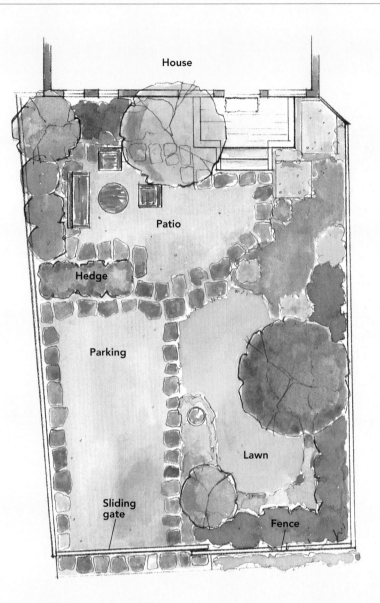

House

Patio

Hedge

Parking

Lawn

Sliding gate

Fence

▲ **Close quarters call for creative solutions.** A pull-in slot provides parking for one car. With a rolling pocket gate, the parking space can be placed close to the street instead of against the house.

▲▲ **A low hedge separates the parking area from the patio,** but matching paving means the parking space can be used for entertaining if the car is moved to the street.

parking area. Yet the parking space, because the materials match those in the patio, can easily double Deborah and Mark Lyon's space for entertaining when the car is parked on the street.

Shrubs soften the lines of the fence, and a small garden filled with roses and perennials brightens the yard through the growing season. A large tree provides a shady canopy and increases the garden's sense of privacy—even though neighboring houses are merely a few feet away.

Street Entries

Gateways are symbolic. They signify an entrance—whether to a ballpark, ranch, garden, or some other realm of existence. In the landscape, they can be functional or merely suggestive. Pillars, gates, wing walls, fences, mailboxes, cairns, and arches can all serve as gateways to let people know they've arrived at the right place. Planting beds can also mark a driveway entry, with or without the aid of structures.

Street-side gateways or entries are both diverse in design and multipurpose in function. In rural areas, gateways at the end of the drive help newcomers find your house, especially if it is hard to see from the road. A gateway sets the tone for the landscape style—be it formal, informal, or otherwise. Consider the metal arch over the gravel entry to a ranch, the cluster of brightly colored annuals by the mailbox of a country cottage, or the imposing stone walls and tall iron gate before an estate.

The most obvious entryway is the gate itself. Gates can be welcoming or austerely off-putting. Though many gates are designed strictly for decorative purposes and left open, others are installed for increased privacy, safety, or improved home security. They can be opened and closed manually or set on an automatic system. They can swing open or, where space is tight, slide into wall or fence pockets. When considering the height and placement of a gate, consult with your building department. Often there are setback requirements, and sometimes permits are required. Also, make sure gates or posts do not obscure the visibility of oncoming traffic. Landscaping around a gate will help tie it into the surrounding yard.

▲ **The simplest gates** can signal an entry.

▼ **Stone pillars mark the gateway to this home,** which has a long, winding driveway and can't be seen from the street. Simple wooden posts or a few sections of split-rail fencing would also serve this role well.

▲Cairns mark the driveway entrance and frame the view of the home. The casualness of these rock formations matches the simple pea-gravel drive.

Pillars, columns, or posts can also mark a driveway entrance. Often they are integrated with a fence or wall that surrounds a property. Other times, they are simply free-standing pillars placed on either side of the driveway. Stacked-stone pillars make a substantial marker. A matching pair of painted wood posts, especially when accompanied by short sections of picket fencing and colorful plantings, can create an elegant entry for a traditional home. Stone posts and a rustic wooden gate would suit a house in the woods or a cabin in the mountains. No matter what type of entry you create, don't forget to post your house numbers where they are clearly visible day and night. And when designing plantings, make sure you're not blocking your view of on-coming traffic.

Property Boundaries

▶Gates can be nicely detailed and offer a glimpse into the garden.

We've all heard the adage, "Good fences make good neighbors" from a Robert Frost poem. But in truth, defining your property boundaries—whether with a fence, wall, hedge, patch of trees, or planting bed—is not so much about your neighbors as it is about you and how you wish to experience and use your front yard. There are as many reasons for defining your periphery as there are ways to do it—to increase privacy, frame pleasing views and screen unwanted ones, define the "walls" of a garden room, provide shelter from prevailing winds, buffer neighborhood noise, keep pets in or out of your yard, and prevent children from running into the street after a stray ball.

For homeowners with small lots, privacy is often a driving force behind enclosing a front yard. Without some sort of buffer, you can often hear your neighbors' conversations or even see into each other's homes. For total privacy, your best bets are tall, solid walls and fences with the pickets or boards spaced very tightly. A dense evergreen hedge will also do the trick, though on a narrow lot, it's important to remember that a hedge occupies much more space than a wall or fence. On larger lots, tall hedges or groves of trees can create a greater sense of privacy.

◀Plant both sides of a fence or wall so your neighbors can enjoy the garden too. A 2- to 4-foot-deep border is all you need for some small shrubs, evergreen perennials, or creeping ground covers. This border is anchored by lavender, with a seasonal planting of nasturtiums at the corner.

5

◄A tall hedge provides ample privacy on a small lot. Here, a formal sheared hedge is most appropriate, as it takes up less space than an informal hedge would.

Nothing will silence a busy street, but masonry walls—and to a lesser degree, hedges and fences—will absorb and reduce traffic noise. The higher the wall the better, because in a built-up area, sound bounces off hard surfaces and can come from many angles other than street level. But keep in mind that sounds will also bounce around inside a masonry wall, so consider softening sections of those walls with vines.

Not all enclosures are the same. You can screen a few areas along your property line with trees, build a high wall to create an enclosed courtyard, or install a low fence over which you can visit with passersby. The material, height, and opacity of your peripheral screening send a message to others about how you want to relate to them. Loose plantings, low walls, and widely spaced picket fences can be very inviting. Tall, solid walls and fences, as well as dense hedges, can be imposing. Even if you prefer your privacy, it's

▲Loose plantings screen utility boxes. Here, the utility box can scarcely be seen (lower left) amid the 'Otto Luyken' laurel. The low, shrubby plantings also provide an attractive, open boundary between the two homes. Closer to the house, taller plants like privet, crape myrtle, and river birch are used for screening.

▲A sheared beech hedge defines a front-yard garden room. The low hedge and open arbor allow neighbors to take a peek at the plantings inside. Graceful ornamental grasses and striking perennials are placed between the hedge and sidewalk to create a "public" garden.

a good idea to send that message in a friendly way. After all, front yards are still considered semipublic areas and contribute to the overall character of a neighborhood. Leave a few feet between your wall, fence, or hedge and the sidewalk for a strip of flowering ground covers or perennials; soften walls or fences with vines; or add some small windows to walls and gates that offer a glimpse inside.

Boundary elements don't have to be high or solid to create a sense of enclosure. Something as simple as a cairn (a small mound of rocks) at each property corner can define your boundaries. A 3-foot wall will allow you to chat freely with neighbors while providing a backdrop for a flower bed. Also, you may choose to partition or screen only one or two sides of your yard, leaving the others open to the street or neighbors' yards.

If you live in a conservative neighborhood and are the first on your block to stake a claim to your front yard by defining your property boundaries, you might consider making changes gradually. Plantings are often more readily

Check Out Local Codes

Local codes and neighborhood covenants regarding walls, fences, and hedges vary. Such guidelines might address the height of walls, the distance a boundary must be placed from the street or curb, and any right-of-way granted to utilities and road crews. Some neighborhoods, in fact, ban any sort of street-side barrier. So before you spend your first nickel, contact your local planning office and homeowners' association, if you have one, to find out what's acceptable and what's not.

When you ask about setback distances, be sure to find out whether the setback is measured from the center of the street or the curb. And double-check the location of your property line—it may be further from the road than you think. Also verify whether the same restrictions apply to hedges, walls, and fences. Often you can grow a hedge where you can't build a permanent structure.

Sometimes there's room for negotiation on codes. If you think you have a strong case, consider applying for a variance. In many places, applying for a variance to build a higher fence or to place it in the right-of-way is considered routine. The application might cost a few hundred dollars and take a few months, but could be worth the cost and effort. A variance is sometimes granted on a conditional basis. For instance, it might state that if the city decides to widen the street, your fence or wall will have to be removed. In that case, you'll simply have to decide whether it's worth the risk.

accepted than walls or fences. Start with a planting bed that runs 15 or 20 feet down the side of your property, perhaps extending from the corners of your house. Anchor this peninsula with a small flowering tree or large shrub, and surround it with a few smaller shrubs, well-behaved perennials, and creeping ground covers. You'll probably find that a few of your neighbors quickly follow suit, and in time, you'll feel more confident expanding the plantings or adding a low fence or wall.

Fences

Wooden fences have long been the screening of choice in America, and for good reason. Throughout much of the country, wood is readily available and therefore affordable. Fences are generally quicker and easier to build than walls, so labor costs are lower as well. And unlike hedges, which need time to grow, fences have immediate impact on the landscape.

Painted fences do need a fresh coat of color every four or five years. Stained fences can often go a bit longer but will look better with a coat from time to time. Wood can also be left to weather naturally, reducing the upkeep. Wooden

▼ **Scalloped picket fences are eye-catching.** They can curve up or down and can be painted to match the color of the house.

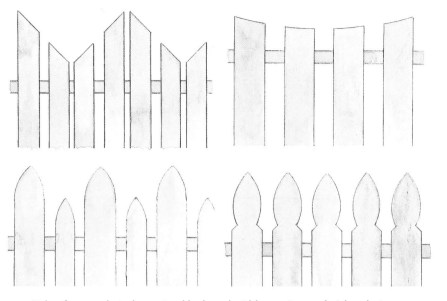

Picket fence style is determined by board width, spacing, and picket designs.

Hoops Add Height to a Fence

A creative technique for increasing the height of a fence is to attach a series of hoops of bent No. 3 rebar to fence posts and train vines up and over them. If your local codes limit fence heights but not plantings, this *may* be a way to add height to your barrier—though you should verify this before adding the hoops. Even if you're restricted in height, extension hoops offer a way to maximize screening without building a high fence.

For good proportion, I like to increase the height of a fence by about half. On a 6-foot fence, for instance, I like to add another 3 feet (measured at the center point) with the hoops. And then to give the fence the perfect finishing touch, I plant flowering vines like climbing roses, jasmine, or honeysuckle along the fence posts and tie them loosely to the hoops as they grow.

fences don't last forever, though. Over the years, pickets and posts may rot, become infested with termites, warp, or fall into general disrepair without regular attention. Still, for the money, they're an excellent form of screening and, with care, can last for many years.

Wood fences come in many styles. Picket fences, the most popular, are commonly found surrounding colonial and cottage homes. Split-rail, running-rail, and board-and-lattice fences are also popular. Of course, fences can be made from materials other than wood. Wrought iron is a favorite in places like New Orleans and Savannah. Bamboo suits oriental gardens and contemporary homes. And fences made of all sorts of metal—from copper and steel to yachting cables—are striking against postmodern architecture. Even chain-link fences, though most often relegated to backyards, can provide affordable and attractive fencing when covered in vines.

You can dress up a fence by mixing construction materials. The easiest way to do this is to build the posts from one material and the fence sections from another. You can also create low base walls from masonry materials, and top them with wood, iron, or metal fences. Just don't mix too many different types of materials.

Another way to dress up a fence is with a gate. Most gates are made from the same materials as the fence itself, though

▲ Though heavy-duty materials were used to construct
this fence, the openness of
the pickets gives it an airy
feeling. A small planting strip
in front of the fence is filled
with low-growing perennials.

▲ Board-and-lattice fences offer privacy on a
corner lot. This cedar fence is nicely detailed
with custom lattice. Leaving spaces between
the boards gives the fence an open, friendly
feel, yet shrubs planted on the inside of the
fence limit views within.

they don't have to be. Continuing the pattern of the fence in
the gate is also common, but by creating a unique gate design with the fence materials, or even changing the materials
themselves, you can call attention to the entry. As an alternative, consider building an arbor or arch over your entry—
with or without a gate—and draping it with a fragrant
climbing rose, favorite clematis, or other twining vine.

▲**A fence both screens the** side yard and provides a solid backdrop for a mixed planting. A latticed window (lower left, next to gate) allows the family dog to keep an eye on front-yard activities.

▶**This picket fence curves** inward at the corner to improve visibility for neighbors backing out of their driveway.

Walls

Walls give a look of permanence to a garden. When well constructed, they are, indeed, long-lasting structures. A solid brick or stone wall may age gracefully for hundreds of years—far outlasting the homeowners. The principal drawback to walls is their initial cost. Both the materials and labor are more expensive than those for fences and hedges. And except for low walls of stacked stone or structural block, you'll probably want to hire a mason, as tall walls require poured-concrete foundations and reinforcing bars. If cost is an issue, you might consider building a small section of wall in a prominent location and establishing remaining boundaries with other materials.

▼**Gates are great places for personalization.** Here, the owner placed a metal cutout of Kokopeli—a mythical figure of the Southwest said to spread music and good cheer — against sticks framed by wrought iron.

Brick and stone are among the most popular wall materials. Stone can be purchased as precisely cut rectangles, roughly quarried rocks, weathered fieldstones, rounded river stones, large ledge stones, and flat flagstones. Colors range from deep terra-cotta to dark gray; some stones even have a metallic sheen. While stone walls over 3 feet should be mortared, short walls may be either mortared or dry stacked. By contrast, all brick walls should be mortared for stability. They can be simply stacked, arranged in patterns, or laid in an open, latticelike fashion. And bricks come in a range of colors—from pale yellow to rusty red to charcoal gray—so you can choose a single color or mix several shades.

Still elegant, but more affordable, are stucco and structural-block walls. Stucco is a colored and textured finish applied over concrete block that can even be built up and rounded off to look like an adobe wall. Capstones or brick trim can add an attractive finishing touch to stucco walls. Structural blocks are oversized, hollow bricks in a wide variety of shapes,

▲A brick wall laid in an open, lattice-like pattern uses fewer bricks and has a lighter feeling. This one has a curved profile, and the solid brick posts are capped with formed concrete finials.

▲ A stacked-stone wall has a been-there-forever look— even if recently constructed. A low wooden gate matches the casual style of the wall.

◄ Mix materials to create a more interesting wall or fence. In the Southwest, rustic stick fencing looks good with adobe and stucco walls.

colors, and finishes that can be used to create single-width, freestanding walls.

An eye-catching gate works just as well with a wall as with a fence and is perhaps even more commonly used with a wall. But unlike fences, walls feature gates made of different materials. Heavy-duty, detailed wooden gates look good with just about any kind of masonry wall; wrought-iron gates are also a good choice. Because solid walls will block any light coming from your house, install some lighting near the gate so guests will feel welcome and you don't have to fumble with your keys in the dark. Arbors are also an option with walls, though they are seen less often. To balance the visual weight of a wall, arbors should be constructed from timbers at least 4 inches thick.

A Wooded Courtyard in the Pacific Northwest

The tall brick wall surrounding this Seattle home is so inviting that passing cars slow to admire it. The brick is nicely detailed—with an attractive cap and inset house numbers. The entry is recessed, with attractive lanterns and a wide brick path that leads from the street to the front door. The Craftsman-style gate is oversized and beautifully detailed, with inviting windows inset across the top. And the entire wall is set back a few feet from the sidewalk; this makes it feel less imposing and also creates a planting strip that has been filled with a lush mix of flowering perennials and shrubs—many of them fragrant. A separate yet equally inviting entrance provides access for family members and friends who park in the driveway. It has a matching gate, along with an arbor built from heavy timbers.

Designed by local landscape architect Keith Geller, the brick wall creates a quiet courtyard. But unlike most courtyards, which consist primarily of paved surfaces, this one features a woodland garden that captures the spirit of the Pacific Northwest. Winding paths of crushed granite make their way through this small forest and to the back yard. Evergreen trees offer additional screening and envelop the space with a sense of serenity. Japanese maples, rhododendrons, and an assortment of perennials accent the garden, while several small water features add to the calm and stillness of the courtyard. A bench allows one to sit and enjoy the setting.

What really makes this work is the attention paid to details. Note the way the bricks are laid in the curving path, the solid construction of the gate and arbor, the natural placement of plants, and the subtlety of the water features.

▶A recessed wall and gate signal the courtyard entry. The custom gate, brick cap, light fixture, and planting strip are all attractive details that make this privacy wall a pleasure to look at.

▲Inside the courtyard, a brick path leads to the front door. The remaining ground has been transformed into a small woodland garden.

▲A masonry wall requires a substantial arbor. This one leads from the driveway to the entry courtyard and extends above the garage doors. In time, it will be softened with vines.

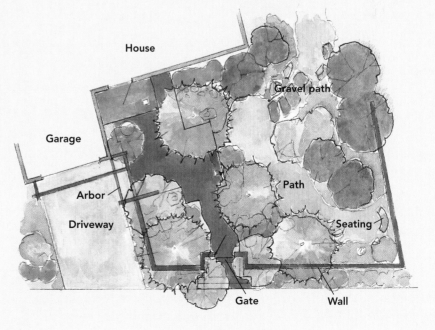

House

Garage

Arbor

Driveway

Gravel path

Path

Seating

Gate

Wall

Hedges

▲ **Even hedges can be used to create a** courtyard. For fun, this homeowner added a corner window for views both into and out of the courtyard garden. Phlox and tulips offer seasonal color in a sidewalk planting strip.

Hedges have many merits. They are less imposing than either walls or fences of equal height and more economical as well. When local codes or neighborhood covenants restrict your use of walls and fences or their height, hedges often offer an acceptable alternative. They can screen views, mitigate strong winds, and create privacy. They can be kept as low as a foot or allowed to soar to more than 10 feet high, depending on your choice of plants and pruning practices. If you select prickly shrubs, they can even serve as an effective barrier. But most delightful of all, they can contribute texture, color, flowers, and even fragrance to the landscape.

Despite their benefits, hedges do have a few drawbacks. First of all, they have to grow—so it may take a few years before they have real impact on the landscape. And because they grow, they need to be pruned. Formal, clipped hedges, in particular, can require attention several times a year. (Informal hedges require only occasional pruning for shape and general plant health.) And finally, hedges take up more room than a wall or fence, a consideration in a narrow space.

Hedges, like other garden elements, are best chosen to match the style of house and garden. A precisely trimmed row of boxwoods will complement a colonial-style home, while a loose hedge of mixed deciduous and evergreen plants might better suit a contemporary house. A softly woven mixture of flowering shrubs of various sizes would enhance the informality of a cottage garden.

Choice Shrubs for Formal Hedges

Arborvitae (*Thuja* spp.)

Beech (*Fagus sylvatica*)

Black bamboo (*Phyllostachys nigra*)

Boxwood (*Buxus sempervirens*)

California wax myrtle (*Myrica californica*)

European hornbeam (*Carpinus betulus*)

Hemlock (*Tsuga* spp.)

Incense cedar (*Calocedrus decurrens*)

Japanese holly (*Ilex crenata*)

Laurustinus (*Viburnum tinus*)

Lavender (*Lavandula* spp.)

Leyland cypress (x *Cupressocyparis leylandii*)

Pittosporum spp.

Privet (*Ligustrum* spp.)

Wax myrtle (*Myrica cerifera*)

Yew (*Taxus* x *media*)

▲ Boxwood

▲ A sheared boxwood hedge suits the formality of this brick colonial. It is kept medium height to echo the boxy shape of the house.

Evergreen plants that respond well to frequent shearing are the best choices for formal hedges. Needled or broad-leaved plants with smaller leaves are easiest to shear. Large-leaved evergreens have to be pruned by hand, as shears will simply clip the leaves in half, leaving the plants looking ragged. Clipped hedges need to look good from top to bottom, so taper them (narrower at the top than bottom) to expose all the branches to sunlight. Otherwise, the lower branches will thin, brown, and die out over the years. For ease of maintenance, keep formal hedges no more than 3 or 4 feet high. Plant in a single row, 1 to 2 feet apart. Planting closely allows the branches to intermingle, one of the distinguishing characteristics of a hedge.

Informal hedges are more laissez-faire, with plants allowed to grow into their natural shape and size. Informal hedges can be one species of evergreen or deciduous shrub, a mix of evergreen or deciduous shrubs, or a tapestry of

▲You don't need a fence or wall to hang a gate. Just place posts on either side of your path next to a hedge or bold plantings, and you can create an eye-catching entry.

evergreen and deciduous shrubs. An evergreen hedge will provide solid, year-round screening. A mixed or deciduous hedge is less dense in winter, but offers seasonal interest with flowers, berries, and colorful foliage.

Shrubs in an informal hedge should be planted farther apart than the same shrubs would be in a formal, clipped hedge. Though the shrubs may be planted in a single row, they create a denser hedge when planted in a staggered row, 2 to 4 feet apart. Because this requires a bed width of at least 8 to 12 feet, staggered hedges are best suited to larger suburban and rural gardens. For a mixed hedge, plant individual shrub types in clusters of three to seven for a stronger visual effect, and repeat the clusters for continuity. One of the tricks to growing a mixed hedge is selecting plants that have similar cultural requirements and are compatible with one another. If one plant is considerably more aggressive than the others, it will soon overwhelm your planting.

Choice Shrubs for Informal Hedges

Alder buckthorn (*Rhamnus frangula* 'Columnaris')
Camellia (*Camellia* spp.)
Cherry and English laurel (*Prunus laurocerasus*)
Common myrtle (*Myrtus communis*)
Escallonia spp.
European cranberry bush (*Viburnum opulus*)
Flowering currant (*Ribes sangvineum*)
Flowering quince (*Chaenomeles* hybrids)
Forsythia x *intermedia*
Glossy abelia (*Abelia* x *grandiflora*)
Hedge maple (*Acer campestre*)
Japanese barberry (*Berberis thunbergii*)
Mock orange (*Philadelphus coronaries*)
Red tip (*Photinia* x *fraseri*)
Rose bay (*Nerium oleander*)
Russian olive (*Elaeagnus angustifolia*)
Rose of Sharon (*Hibiscus syriacus*)
Shrub roses (*Rosa* spp.)
Viburnum spp.
Weigela spp.

▲ Barberry

▶ **In an informal hedge,** plants are allowed to grow into their natural form rather than sheared into geometric shapes. This one, filled with repeat-blooming landscape roses, creates a gently curving border along the property line.

Periphery Plantings

As an alternative to hedges, mixed plantings may be used to mark your property boundary. Unlike hedges, which are composed strictly of shrubs, mixed plantings may include trees, shrubs, perennials, and other plants. And instead of being planted in rows, mixed plantings are usually placed in loose, curving island beds for a more natural look. Though the subject of plantings will be covered more thoroughly in Chapter 8, we'll take a brief look here at their use to delineate property boundaries.

One benefit of a mixed planting is the ease with which you can both screen unwanted views and preserve desirable views. Taller and broader plants can be grown for screening, and lower plantings can continue a bed while preserving a view. You can even leave gaps between two or more taller plantings, such as the limbs of trees, to frame especially inviting views.

▼A large, partially wooded lot deserves an attractive mixed planting along its border. This one includes an understory of dogwoods and azaleas.

▲Mixed plantings work in smaller spaces too, such as this narrow strip between neighboring driveways. Simply use smaller trees and shrubs, and plant them densely.

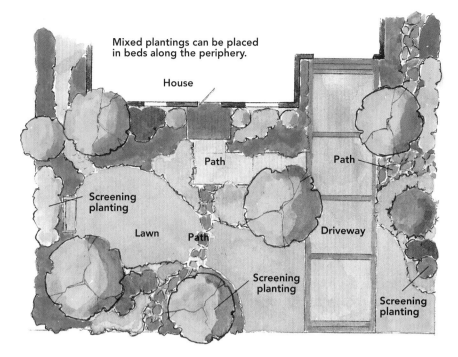

Mixed plantings can be placed in beds along the periphery.

House

Path

Path

Screening planting

Lawn

Path

Driveway

Screening planting

Screening planting

◄A wooded front yard can be transformed into a shady destination. Clear the underbrush to create winding trails and sitting areas. Even though it's in a subdivision, this home feels more secluded.

Mixed plantings can be low or high, open or dense, depending on whether you need solid screening or simply want to mark your periphery. You don't need a large area to exercise your horticultural muscle. A bed just 6 feet wide by 10 feet long has plenty of room for a small tree, a few low shrubs, and an assortment of perennials. Think about how the planting will look from all sides—for what your neighbor sees is just as important as what you see. Though all rules are meant to be broken at one time or another, it's a good idea to place the trees toward the middle of the bed, surround them with shrubs, and then use perennials, bulbs, and ground covers to fill around the edges. When you place your tallest plants slightly off center, your planting will look more natural.

If you are blessed with a wooded lot, think about leaving a buffer of trees between your yard and your neighbor's, or even between your house and the street.

A Cottage Garden for a Corner Lot

Bob McIntyre always wanted a house with a picket fence, and he finally got his wish. His house sits at an intersection in Palo Alto, California, where local codes restrict peripheral fences to 3 feet tall at corners and require a 2-foot setback from the sidewalk so oncoming vehicles are visible. He started with a 3-foot, curved-top picket fence and added an arbor where it wouldn't interfere with visibility. The setback left just enough space to plant a lavender border. Nasturtiums are tucked in at the corner, and roses scramble up the arbor, making a colorful splash every summer. The fence and plantings have since spurred the creation of other boisterous front-yard gardens throughout the neighborhood.

Though the fence is low, it gives a sense of protection from the sidewalk and street. It is neighbor-friendly, allowing passersby to view the garden when they are out for an evening walk. The garden is laid out on an axis, with a brick main path and grassy side path. Each path has a focal point—a birdbath for the main path, and a bench flanked by lemon trees for the side path.

▲ **A 3-foot-tall picket fence set back 2 feet from the sidewalk** offers privacy on this corner lot without obstructing views of oncoming traffic. And the bright, prolific plantings are a hallmark of cottage garden design.

▲**Paths placed on axis are surrounded with lush plantings,** and a bench offers a place to sit in warm weather.

▶**Near the front door, the entry area was** extended with a small brick terrace. A window box, container plantings, and wicker chair make it inviting.

Bob often sits on the bench to read the paper and watch life in the neighborhood. We also built a small brick terrace near the front door, but the wicker chair there is more for looks than anything else. (Bob prefers sitting on the bench, which is further from the street.)

The garden is a riot of color all season long. The deep red roses Bob planted by the arbor are the queens of the garden in late spring, while masses of black-eyed Susans step up to the starring role in summer. They are tempered by wine-foliaged plants such as smokebush, New Zealand flax, and 'Chameleon' spurge. Cannas, dahlias, and lobelia jazz up the plantings with their bright red flowers, while window boxes, container plantings, and an herb garden bring life to the terrace.

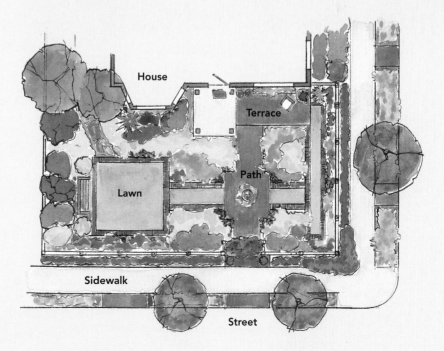

Foundation Plantings

▶**This neat and trim foundation planting** loosens up as the bed extends beyond the house.

Houses haven't always had foundation plantings. The practice of planting evergreen shrubs around the base of a house became popular when builders started using concrete block for foundations instead of brick or stone. Concrete block was cheaper and easier to install but wasn't very attractive. So foundation plantings as we know them evolved primarily as a way to hide part of the house.

Without foundation plantings, many houses would simply look like big boxes set down on a flat surface—what is sometimes called "plop architecture." Foundation plantings help soften that look, tying a house to the surrounding landscape and giving it a sense of belonging. Foundation plants can also help a house feel less imposing, especially large houses. Trees, shrubs, and vines break up broad expanses of wall and offer intimate details—such as the perfume of a rose or the delicate tracery of a Japanese maple leaf—that can be appreciated up close. Plants can draw your eye to a door, bay window, or other interesting architectural feature. And their greenery gives a sense of life and vitality to a house. In essence, foundation plantings can make a house more inviting.

◀**Foundation plantings can be colorful. Start with flowering evergreen shrubs and then add** deciduous shrubs, perennials, and annuals for additional seasonal color.

▲ Foundation plantings don't have to be evergreen or shrubby. This house is surrounded by upright grasses, mounding perennials, and spreading ground covers. Boulders are placed for accent, helping the home settle into its Rocky Mountain surroundings.

The act of placing plants around the base of a house is a little like dressing a person. Some homes can get away with a short skirt of plant material but most look best with a little more cover—perhaps a mix of larger shrubs and even a few trees. How we go about cloaking our homes depends a lot on their shape, size, and architectural style. Some are complemented by a casual arrangement of loose plantings; others are best suited to a tailored look—evenly trimmed hedges with matching architectural accessories.

Though it's common to simply plant a row of evergreens from one end of the house to the other, foundation plantings are more interesting if they feature a variety of plants—both evergreen and deciduous—and range in height from creeping ground covers to upright trees.

▲ A single striking plant, such as this white-flowering spirea, has the ability to unify a group of town houses or a neighborhood.

Evergreen Foundation Plants

PERENNIALS

African blue lily	*Agapanthus* 'Storm Cloud'
Big blue lily turf	*Liriope muscari*
Christmas fern	*Polysticum arostichoides*
Hellebore	*Helleborus* spp.
Japanese rush	*Acorus gramineus* 'Ogon'
Pheasant's tail grass	*Stipa arundinacea*

▲ *Agapanthus*

SHRUBS

Chinese juniper	*Juniperus chinensis*
Common boxwood	*Buxus sempervirens*
Common camellia	*Camellia japonica*
Cherry laurel	*Prunus laurocerasus*
Heavenly bamboo	*Nandina domestica*
Japanese holly	*Ilex crenata* 'Convexa'
Japanese mock orange	*Pittosporum tobira* 'Wheeler's Dwarf'
Pieris	*Pieris* 'Forest Flame'
Rhododendron	*Rhododendron* spp.
Sweetbox	*Sarcococca hookeriana*

TREES

African fern pine	*Africarpus gracilior*
American arborvitae	*Thuja occidentalis*
Brazilian pepper tree	*Schinus terebinthifolius*
Bronze loquat	*Eriobotrya deflexa*
Columnar yew	*Taxus x media* 'Hicksii'
Nellie Stephens holly	*Ilex* 'Nellie R. Stephens'
New Zealand tea tree	*Leptospermum scoparium*
Sweet bay	*Laurus nobilis*
Sweet olive	*Osmanthus fragrans*

◀ **Not all houses have foundations to hide.** Sometimes low-growing ground covers like pachysandra are much more pleasing than shrubs. Deciduous trees with bright red berries like this crabapple are a pleasure to view from house windows and attract birds in winter.

Architectural Cues

Foundation plants should complement the style, lines, and scale of a house. Take a close look at your house to determine its overriding style. If the house is symmetric, plantings should match on either side of the door. As you move away from the center of the house, you can either continue to match the plantings or gradually introduce some variation. Overall, however, the plantings should be balanced. In addition to balance, most symmetric homes look best with geometrically arranged and neatly manicured plantings. That doesn't mean shearing shrubs into matching meatballs, but formal homes do benefit from an overall sense of uniformity.

Asymmetric houses offer more freedom in plant selection and placement. Balance still plays a role, but the rules have changed. Instead of simply balancing plantings with each other, you are sometimes balancing plantings with architectural features. For instance, if the chimney rises above the

▼**Symmetry calls for simplicity.** Just match the plantings on either side of the house. Formal plantings of boxwood and topiaries are softened with cosmos and lavender.

Plantings accent and balance an asymmetrically designed house.

Matched plantings suit a symmetrically designed house.

roofline on one side of the house, a conifer planted on the other side that peaks just above the roofline would suggest a sense of balance. But rather than worry too much about creating balance, concentrate instead on establishing natural-looking mixed plantings that frame the house and highlight its architectural features.

Plants can also highlight the architectural lines of a house. A low sheared hedge along the base of a ranch-style house will emphasize its horizontal profile. Columnar trees placed at the corners will accent a tall, narrow house. Big boxwoods on either side of a front door will echo the mass of a boxy house. It is possible, however, to have too much of a good thing: For visual interest, include a few plants with contrasting shapes to break those same lines. Two small columnar plants on either side of the front door will break the strong horizontal lines of the ranch-style house. Several large, rounded, or horizontal shrubs beneath the windows of the tall house will bring your view back down to eye level. Clusters of differently shaped and sized plants at the corners of the boxy house will make it feel less overpowering.

Also remember to keep the scale of the house in mind when choosing plants. Tall trees may anchor a two-story house, but those same trees would dwarf a cottage. Here,

◄**A large house needs deep foundation beds.** This one features layered plantings that ease the transition from rooftop to ground plane. A beautifully shaped maple anchors the corner, while a mix of evergreen and deciduous shrubs fill in beneath. Perennials and ornamental grasses complete the composition.

▼**A tall evergreen holly draws your attention** toward the door, but these flowering mophead hydrangeas are clearly the showstoppers in spring.

small ornamental trees would be a much better choice. Similarly, homes with several feet of exposed foundation need more massive foundation shrubs than homes built on slab with little or no exposed foundation.

Foundation plants can call attention to or play down the architectural features of a house. The most important architectural element to highlight is the front door. You can do this by placing slightly taller plants on either side of the stoop or landing. If the doorway and mantel are symmetric—matching lanterns or window panels on either side—the plantings immediately to either side of the door are usually matched, even if the house is asymmetric and the remaining foundation plantings are informal. Asymmetric doorways—those with a window panel or light fixture on just one side—can be treated either formally or informally. A combined approach can also be effective: Place a balanced, mixed planting on either side of the doorway but vary the plants in those groupings.

Plant form is as important as plant placement in creating focus on a doorway. Both plant height and shape are factors to be considered. Hard lines and strong form attract attention; softer shapes are less commanding. As a general rule, strong geometric forms are most appropriate for formal

Establishing Grade

For healthy plant growth and a dry basement, you need good drainage around the base of your house. If water tends to settle around the foundation rather than draining away from it, you can just about count on a moldy environment and a leaking or flooded basement in heavy rainfall. This excess moisture can also hurt plants. Soil that retains too much water prevents plant roots from absorbing oxygen—and this leads to root rot, which will harm and eventually kill many plants.

The soil line should be at least 6 inches below the base of the wall framing to prevent dampness and dry rot in your home. From there, the soil should slope steadily away from the house—a 5 percent grade for the first 6 feet is recommended. The runoff from gutters also needs to be directed away from the house. This water can be channeled down a slope where it can settle naturally into the soil, or into a swale or dry stream toward your neighborhood's storm-drainage system.

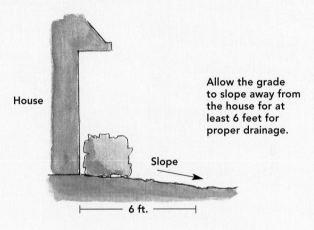

House

Allow the grade to slope away from the house for at least 6 feet for proper drainage.

Slope

├─── 6 ft. ───┤

Homes built on a slab foundation need only minimal foundation plantings.

homes, while softer shapes suit informal houses. In a formal setting, matching round or conical shrubs could be placed either side of the door, in most cases extending no more than three-quarters the height of the door. In an informal setting, something softer, and often taller, is nice. A small tree, such as a dogwood (*Cornus* spp.) or vine maple (*Acer circinatum*), could create a canopy over or near the doorway.

▲ Anchor your house corner with an elegant tree. This redbud has flowers in spring, flat pods in summer, colorful foliage in fall, and an interesting trunk and branching pattern in winter.

A climbing rose trained up and over the door, would also be a good choice.

Beyond the front door, the corners of a house usually demand the most attention. This is where your house meets the surrounding landscape, and plantings serve as a visual anchor. The traditional approach is to place tall evergreens at the corners. This softens the hard lines along the edges of your house. The key is giving those evergreens space to grow without rubbing against the walls and eaves. It's also possible to place taller plantings further away from the house, with only a low planting at the corner.

Foundation plantings can also point out special architectural details, such as a bay window or stacked-stone wall. A small stone wall, for example, can be framed along its base and sides, but a large wall might better serve as an attractive, textural backdrop for a striking specimen plant. *Azara*, which has a charming arching habit, glossy green leaves, and scented flowers in late winter and early spring, would be a good choice. So would an espaliered firethorn (*Pyracantha* spp.) or fruit tree.

To accent a bay window, you might simply bring a low ground cover planting or paving material up to the foundation wall. Taller plants on either side of the window would make a nice accent. If you prefer something lush, plant a low hedge at the base of the window, and train a climbing rose or other flowering vine up one angle of the bay. Bay windows, because they are so open and inviting, are especially suited for nearby floral displays, shrubs with winter berries, or trees with interesting foliage. If some screening is desired from indoors, consider planting a small tree, such as a crape myrtle (*Lagerstroemia* spp.) or Japanese maple (*Acer palmatum*), outside your bay window.

Not all houses need plants skirting their entire foundation. If you have a handsome brick or stone foundation, you might want to show it off in sections. Or if your home is built on a slab foundation, you may find some breaks in the plantings refreshing. Clustering plantings near doorways, corners, and other architectural features may be enough. But most of us have less-than-attractive foundations, and planting low shrubs beneath windows is a good way to screen them.

▲ **Fragrance is a bonus in foundation plantings,** especially near an entry. This evergreen planting includes the herbs lavender, rosemary, germander, and thyme.

▶ **Turn foundations into mixed borders**—especially beneath windows where you can enjoy them from inside as well as outside. Just be sure to pay as much attention to plant form and foliage as you do to the fleeting flowers when making your selections.

A Foundation Renovation

When Anne and Dave Hall moved into their two-story colonial five years ago, the ground floor of the house was obscured by what the neighbors called "the mounds"—huge junipers that had outgrown their allotted space. While many homeowners would simply let them be—after all, tackling giant, prickly junipers can be daunting—the Halls bit the bullet and ripped them out.

Since Anne was new to gardening, she recruited designer Lisa Ravenholt to help her select replacement plants. Together, they came up with a striking combination—upright junipers for accent, a line of dwarf boxwood edging the front of the beds for year-round form and color, and a mix of evergreen and deciduous shrubs and perennials to fill in the middle. Roses, hydrangeas, and perennials brighten the

▲ **Not-so-traditional foundation plantings surround this traditional home.** Dwarf boxwoods contribute a sense of formality, while looser plantings soften the composition. Taller plants frame the doorway and anchor the corners.

beds in spring and summer, while the lustrous red berries of heavenly bamboo add a splash of color in fall and winter. A saucer magnolia anchors the corner; as it grows, it will offer its lovely blossoms each spring. The clipped evergreens surrounding the looser plantings give the foundation planting a sense of exuberant order.

To keep their budget realistic, the Halls started with very small plants. But as you can see, they've filled in nicely in just five years. Starting small also allows plants to become well adapted to their conditions. A few plantings remained on the property—like the 20-year-old espaliered pear next to the garage. Unlike the ridiculed old junipers, the espalier has inspired many neighbors to have a go at creating their own. And now, perhaps, the new foundation plantings will be inspiration as well.

▲ **Instead of being placed against the house,** evergreen shrubs are put at the front of the bed to give this planting a sense of order.

◀ **This 20-year-old espaliered pear** is a focal point in the front yard, flanking the house side of the detached garage.

Bed Layout

Foundation beds need not be straight and narrow; give yourself more space in which to plant. The easiest way to do this is to simply make existing foundation beds deeper—bringing them farther out from the house. In most cases, you can easily increase the depth by half, and often you can double it. If your existing foundation plants are in good shape, you can use them as a backdrop for other plantings. For instance, if you have a row of evergreen shrubs beneath your windows, you can add clusters of ornamental grasses, long-flowering perennials, and evergreen ground covers, along with seasonal bulbs and annuals, in front of them.

Instead of a straight border, you might give yours generous curves. Allow it to cross over paths and move out into the lawn. Curving beds are more suitable for clusters of shrubs and perennials and masses of ground covers. A bed that curves outward as it moves toward the corners of the house offers another benefit—especially for homes built on a central axis. You can plant formal rows of shrubs near the front door and against the house, but loosen up the plantings as you move away from the door by planting clusters of smaller shrubs or perennials in front of them.

Extend the foundation plantings in peninsula-like fashion from the corners of the house—like arms reaching out, embracing the yard. Once again, curve the beds to make them look more natural, and then fill them with mixed plantings—such as a dogwood surrounded by a cluster of azaleas and edged with perennials, spring bulbs, and ferns. To complete the design, place a stepping-stone path through

▲ **This foundation bed curves gently,** which suits the natural surroundings well. Beds are filled with rhododendrons, azaleas, and other evergreen shrubs, as well as a few Japanese maples for leaf contrast and seasonal interest.

Cultural Conditions Unique to Foundations

Chances are, the soil surrounding the foundation of your house is considerably different from the soil elsewhere in your yard. That's because this area is excavated during construction, often backfilled with poor-quality soil, and then compacted. This creates a problem for plants that need to send their roots deep into the soil for nourishment. There is also a good chance that the soil around the base of your house is more alkaline because of leaching that occurs from cement foundations. The bottom line is that the soil around a foundation almost always needs to be loosened and amended before planting. Whether it is predominantly sand, clay, or some other base, it will benefit from compost worked in as deeply as possible. A soil test will provide guidelines for adjusting the nutrient content and pH.

The other thing to keep in mind with foundation plants is that, if placed beneath a deep eave, they may not receive the same amount of rainfall as the other plants in your garden. Either plant beyond the eave or consider installing a simple irrigation system to ensure that they receive ample moisture.

▲ **This foundation bed has been expanded to serve as a focal point** in the landscape. Colorful flowers can be easily seen through the bay window.

◄ **Consider expanding your planting area by broadening** foundation beds as they move away from the front door. To keep beds and lawns from starting a turf battle, edge your beds with brick or stone.

▲ **Beds can reach out from the corners** of the house toward the street to loosely enclose a front yard. Planting a tree or two in these beds can create a little shade for understory shrubs and woodland perennials.

the bed for easy access to the side yard or a neighbor's home. These extended, peninsula-like foundation beds are an excellent way to integrate a house with the surrounding landscape and create a greater sense of privacy in a front yard.

Be sure to leave a little space between your plantings and your house, as well as a path to access this space. It's not much fun brushing branches aside every time you need to turn on the water, prune your shrubs, or wash your windows. Both your family and the utility meter readers will appreciate the gesture.

Three-Dimensional Plantings

All plants exhibit form. Some reach up, tall and branching; others remain low and creeping; some can even be pruned into tight geometric forms. Your goal is to have an interesting mix of shapes without going overboard—three or four distinct forms are usually sufficient.

Before you go shopping at the nursery, try thinking about plants as three-dimensional objects—boxes, cones, balls, and other shapes. As an exercise, get a small box shaped roughly like your house, and try placing objects in front of it as if they were foundation plants. Common items from the kitchen make excellent doubles for plants and help you think about their shape. Turn a catsup bottle into a conifer, an orange into a round shrub, a spaghetti box into a low

▼ **Combine different plant shapes for visual contrast.** No shrubs are naturally square, but boxwoods are round. Upright clumps of variegated lilyturf have a fountainlike habit, while this Japanese maple displays a horizontal spreading form.

A Variety of Shapes

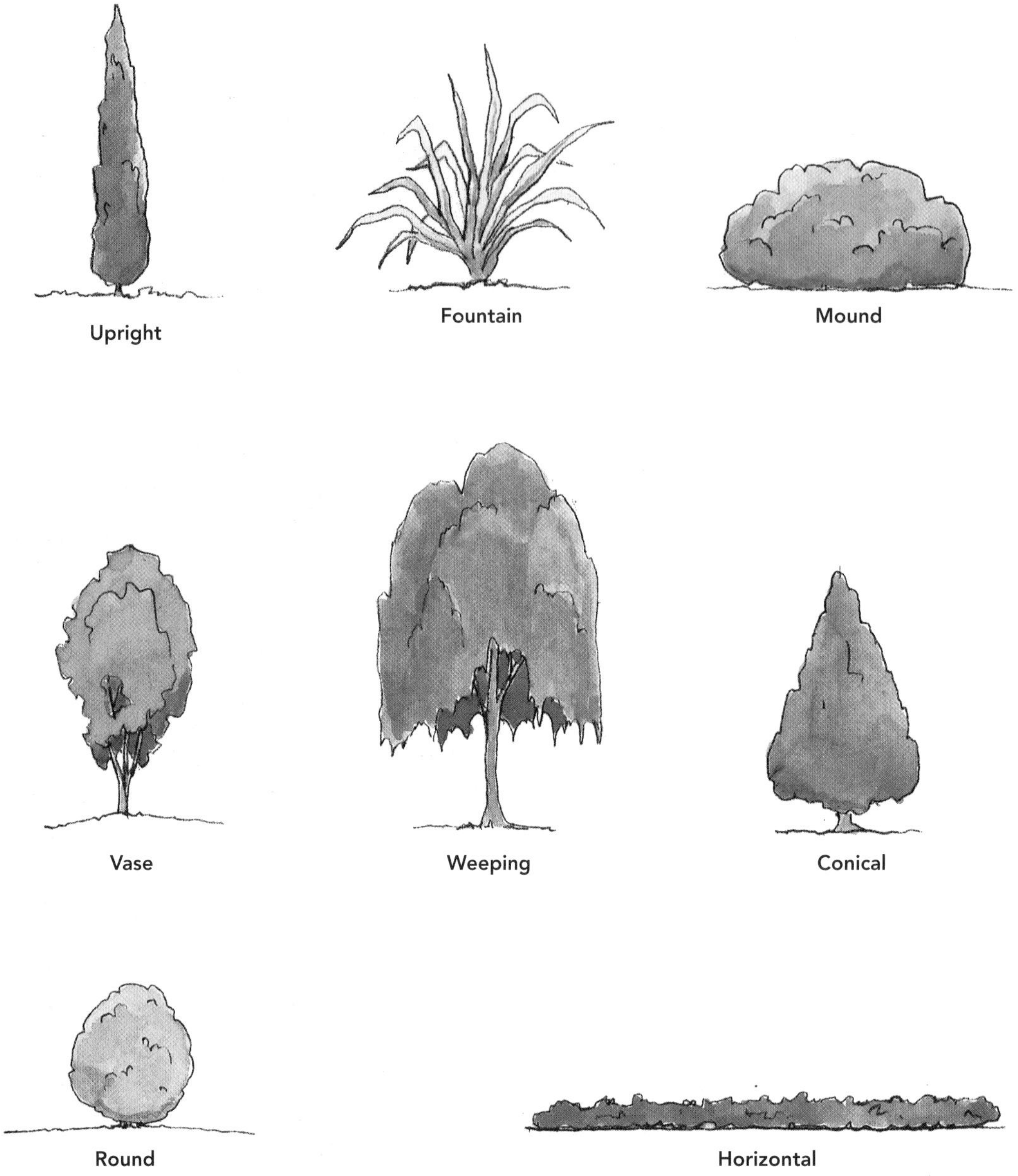

Upright

Fountain

Mound

Vase

Weeping

Conical

Round

Horizontal

hedge, and a wineglass into a tree. Move the objects around until you have a pleasing arrangement.

And finally, relate these shapes to plants. Some plants, such as hollies (*Ilex* spp.) and boxwood (*Buxus* spp.), look good pruned into spheres on either side of a stoop or sheared into rectangular hedges beneath a row of windows. Others, such as Italian cypress (*Cupressus sempervirens*) or 'Hicksii' yews (*Taxus* x *media* 'Hicksii'), have a naturally upright, columnar form suited to house corners or framing doors. And still others have loose, informal forms that look

▲ **This foundation planting** includes two rows of evergreen shrubs. The rhododendrons at the back have a loose habit and large leaves, while the boxwoods in the front have small leaves and adapt easily to shaping or shearing.

▲ **Deep beds offer plenty of planting opportunities.** Grow taller trees or vines next to the house as a backdrop, and shorter plants toward the front edge next to the lawn. It's a good idea to include at least some evergreens for year-round structure.

good in clusters. Within each shape category there will always be many plants that offer a variety of texture, color, fragrance, and seasonal interest.

A key to creating interesting plantings is to plant dimensionally—that is, to consider the different layers available in the space. Applied to foundation plantings, you have the space against the house wall, the area on the ground, and that roughly triangular area between the two to work with.

It's this middle layer that we tend to think of as the shrub layer. This is the primary planting layer designed principally to complement the architecture of the house. Though evergreen shrubs will provide year-round color and structure, consider mixing in a few deciduous shrubs for their winter berries, spring flowers, or fall leaves.

Neat and Trim Traditional

If you walk through this quiet northern Georgia neighborhood in the evening, you're likely to see Marian or Gene Burch in their front yard. Because the yard is surrounded by mixed plantings with an assortment of trees and shrubs along the periphery, the front yard has a cozy, inviting feeling—though it's anything but small or secluded. They inherited most of the plantings from previous owners, but enjoy tucking in annuals for an extra splash of color

and taking time to appreciate the landscape roses that bloom repeatedly throughout the summer along the driveway.

The house was built around five years ago, so the shrubs and trees in the foundation plantings haven't quite reached maturity. Even so, they have filled in nicely and do an admirable job connecting the house to the surrounding landscape. The designer used a mix of evergreen and deciduous trees—some with single trunks, and others

▲ From a distance, these foundation plantings look neat and trim—though they offer much more variety than a row of sheared evergreen shrubs.

◄**These foundation plantings are layered,** especially at the corners of the house—from trees and shrubs to low-growing perennials. Spirea adds a splash of color in summer.

that are multitrunked—to anchor the corners of the house and to provide shade near key windows. Shrubs, too, are a blend of deciduous and evergreen, and the spirea blooms for long periods in summer. There are other reasons the foundation plantings fit the house so well. First, though many different plants are used, most shrubs and perennials are planted in masses, and some of these masses are repeated in more than one location. And second, the layering from ornamental trees to shrubs, and then to perennials and the lawn, makes a smooth, natural transition.

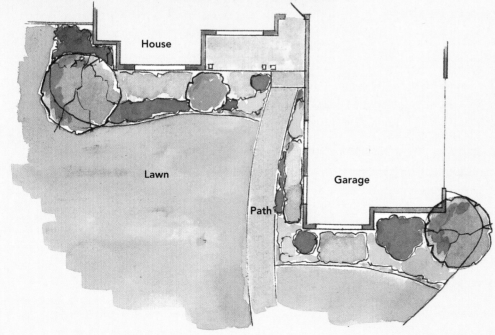

House

Lawn

Path

Garage

Deciduous Shrubs With Multiseason Interest

Azaleas	*Rhododendron* spp.	Meyer lilac	*Syringa meyeri*
Burning bush	*Euonymus alatus* 'Rudy Haag'	Purple beautyberry	*Callicarpa dichotoma*
Chinese snowball	*Viburnum macrocephalum*	Redtwig dogwood	*Cornus alba* 'Sibirica'
Dwarf forsythia	*Forsythia* 'Arnold Dwarf'	Rockspray cotoneaster	*Cotoneaster horizontalis*
Dwarf fothergilla	*Fothergilla major* 'Mount Airy'	Shrub roses	*Rosa* spp.
Hydrangeas	*Hydrangea* spp.	Snowmound spirea	*Spiraea nipponica* 'Snowmound'
Japanese barberry	*Berberis thunbergii*	Virginia sweetspire	*Itea virginica* 'Henry's Garnet'

The house façade offers an often-neglected planting opportunity. By planting something tall on or against a wall, you create a greater sense of depth in your foundation plantings and bring life to a space that is usually barren. A wall is the perfect backdrop for a tree with an interesting branching pattern, especially when you place low landscape lights in front of the tree to bathe it with light, casting interesting shadows on the wall behind. A wall is also an ideal surface for a climbing vine.

When it comes to foundation plantings, the ground plane is often overlooked as well. Bringing the bed out further, as previously mentioned, will give you more space to add an interesting ground-cover layer. To create strength in the bed line, edge it with flat stones or brick; this also makes it easier to mow the lawn. Evergreen ground covers, small ornamental grasses, geraniums (*Pelargonium* spp.), and all sorts of small, spreading, or clumping perennials can be planted in this area. Choose a bright-foliaged plant like Bowles' golden sedge (*Carex elata* 'Aurea') or Japanese rush (*Acorus gramineus* 'Ogon') to contrast with a darker evergreen backdrop. Select a bold-foliaged plant like *Hosta* or lambs' ears (*Stachys byzantina*) as a contrast to the lawn. Or add life to the plantings with clusters of feather reed grass (*Calamagrostis acutiflora*) that blow in even the gentlest of breezes.

▲The easiest way to improve a traditional foundation planting of a row of evergreen shrubs is to bring the bed out far enough to add a few perennials.

Plant Selection

Another key to creating an interesting planting bed is to include a variety of plant types—trees, shrubs, perennials, annuals, ground covers, and spring bulbs. When you vary the plant types, your foundation plantings will come to life and change with the seasons. Start with those that provide structure—a solid backdrop in any season, as well as defined shapes that relate to the lines and architectural features of the house. Evergreens are usually the best choices for these positions, but deciduous plants can also contribute structure, in winter as well as summer.

The easiest way to create visual interest is to add contrast in the garden, though too much contrast will just make your foundation plantings look busy. The secret to achieving the right balance is massing—grouping or clustering several of the same plants—and varying the size of those masses. Though single plants can be used, they are most often used for accent—perhaps at the doorway or house corner. Not every plant can be the star of the show; most will play supporting roles. Among the qualities to look for when select-

▼ **Different leaf colors provide visual interest**—especially with the yellow-variegated hostas and burgundy-leaved coralbells. The lacy foliage of ferns also contrasts with the bold leaves of the hostas.

ing plants for a well-rounded foundation planting are contrasting

- **Leaf shapes and sizes**—from fine-needled to broad, ovate to palmate
- **Leaf textures**—from prickly to soft, coarse to smooth
- **Plant form**—from rounded or conical to sprawling or fountainlike
- **Height**—from ground-hugging to towering
- **Foliage color**—from dark, glossy green to pale green, and even variegated or colored leaves

Evergreens provide year-round structure, but deciduous plants help us celebrate seasonal changes. Both trees and shrubs may offer flowers, berries, and changing foliage through the seasons, and also good nesting sites for birds. Flowering bulbs, perennials, vines, and ground covers can offer almost continuous color and fragrance in the garden—even through winter if we select carefully.

Balance your plant choices so each season is represented. And give priority to plants that have multiseason interest, such as ornamental trees. In spring, they will display their lovely flowers; in summer, they provide shade from the hot sun. In fall, their changing leaves will brighten a nearby room with color. In winter, their bare branches allow sunshine to warm your house.

▲**Showcase the seasons.** Fleabane and Jerusalem sage offer a profusion of flowers in summer; *Rosa glauca* showcases its pink flowers and burgundy foliage until replaced by orange-red hips in fall. Smokebush features both deeply colored leaves and smoky plumes. Dwarf evergreen boxwood gives this planting year-round structure.

Updating Existing Plantings

Whether you've inherited foundation plantings from a previous homeowner or just need to spruce up some mature plantings, it's a good idea to carry a checklist with you to the garden for evaluation. Here's what you'll need to look at:

• Health—Overall, how do the plants look? Are they full and vibrant, or do they look lean, as if struggling for sunlight? Does the foliage look healthy, or is it yellowing, diseased, or infested with pests? If the plantings look pretty healthy overall, are there individual plants that show less vigor?

• Form—Does the overall planting style suit the house? Do individual plants accent architectural features or serve some other role? Is there variety in form, or are all the plants the same shape and size?

• Size—Are the plants in scale with the house? Have some plants grown too large, perhaps covering up windows or blocking paths?

• Texture and colors—Do the plant colors harmonize with each other and with the house? Is there enough variety in foliage and flower color? Or perhaps too much variety?

Once you've completed your evaluation, you can begin to redesign your plantings and address the needs of individual plants. If, overall, your plantings are well designed but don't look very healthy, start with a soil test. You might discover that all you need is a good boost of chelated iron or some other nutrient. If it's not that, perhaps your plants are too sheltered and need more water, or maybe it's too shady, and you need to thin out the canopy of nearby trees. Seriously damaged or diseased plants should probably be removed, but

▲ **Varied foliage color and texture make all-evergreen** plantings more interesting. Just be sure to select plants that mature at heights you consider acceptable in your foundation. Otherwise, you'll need to spend a lot of time with the pruning shears to keep them in shape.

whenever possible, try to salvage plants—either pruning them or moving them to a new location. Except with young plants, pruning is almost always easier than transplanting. In some cases, however, it's easier just to remove an existing plant and start fresh with another one that better suits the site.

If your problems are design-oriented, think about how you would create new plantings from scratch, and then see which existing plants might be adapted in some way to that plan. In many cases, you may just need to add plants for variety—working in a small tree or a few deciduous shrubs, extending the bedlines from the corner of the house, or making the beds deeper to add some clusters of smaller shrubs, perennials, and ground covers.

Ground Covers

▶Edging laid a foot or more wide can double as a narrow garden path when the grass is wet.

When we think of ground covers for the residential landscape, we usually think of lawns. And for outdoor activities, lawns just might be the perfect surface. They're ideal for ball games, picnics, or a game of tag. They serve admirably as a spot for yard sales and garden parties. Babies take their first steps on cushioned lawns, and a few years later, can be seen sitting on those patches of grass blowing dandelions into the wind.

But lawns aren't, and shouldn't be, our only choice for ground covers. They are only suitable for sites that receive plenty of sunlight and climates with ample rainfall, and even there, they are quite demanding— just look at how much time and money we spend mowing, blowing, raking, weeding, aerating, dethatching, reseeding, patching, fertilizing, and treating lawns. A better model for front-yard landscaping is to use mown

lawns where they can be enjoyed, admired, and easily maintained, and to cover other areas with lower-maintenance alternatives such as creeping evergreen perennials, masses of low-growing shrubs, mulches, and paved surfaces. In fact, these other ground covers can help set off a lawn, improving its overall looks and impact in the landscape.

Some of the most beautiful front yards are those with a combination of different ground covers. To decide which

◀Varying the ground covers gives a yard a tapestry look that is very appealing. Here, a well-defined and edged lawn is surrounded by evergreen lilyturf, which both flowers and bears berries.

◄Clearly defining edges makes lawns look much neater; they're also easier to mow.

►Periwinkle grows easily and spreads quickly to create a solid mat beneath deciduous trees. In spring, it is covered with pale lavender flowers.

ground cover goes where, divide your yard into zones of activity. For instance, you might have zones for high-impact activities like touch football and playing with the family dog, and zones for low-impact activities such as sitting on a bench, playing quiet games, or dining with friends. You'll have zones where you rarely, if ever, spend time, as well as zones for circulation. Also, note areas with heavy shade or full sun, or that are too steep to tend.

Lawns have the most uniform surface and can withstand foot traffic. They're ideal for spaces devoted to high-impact activities. Their fine texture and uniformity is also a nice contrast to most other garden plants, so they are effective in setting off a flower bed or border. Because most turf grasses prefer full sun, lawns are not a good choice for shady areas, such as beneath large trees or on the north side of a house. While they require ample moisture, they don't like to have their roots standing in water—so low-lying areas that tend to puddle are best covered with something else. And finally, because they have to be mowed regularly (weekly or more often during their growing season), lawns are problematic on steep slopes where mowing would be dangerous.

▲Pachysandra and periwinkle are both suited to shade and can handle some sun. They are great alternatives where lawn refuses to flourish, or where the terrain makes it difficult to mow.

Other low-growing plants not only serve as alternatives to lawn in these trouble spots but can cover low-traffic areas—especially those along the periphery of your property. Small clumping plants and ornamental grasses are ideal for compact areas, while plants that spread quickly by long runners or stems are better for large areas. Shade-tolerant ground covers work well beneath trees or adjacent to a house. And mass plantings of low-growing shrubs can be striking in the landscape. Often, the best choice is a nonliving ground cover—mulch, chipped gravel, or other paving material. These are suited to high-traffic areas and spaces for dining and outdoor entertainment.

Before heading to the store for ground covers, think back to your site evaluation. What did you discover about your yard that will affect your ground cover selections? You'll also want to assess your maintenance and budget concerns. Here are some of the issues to think through:

• **Climate**—Most lawns and many plants need substantial water and are not good choices for drought-prone

Ground-Cover Zones

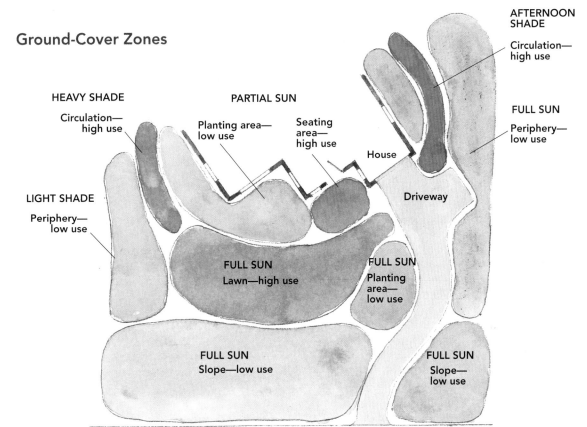

AFTERNOON SHADE
Circulation—high use

HEAVY SHADE
Circulation—high use

PARTIAL SUN

FULL SUN
Periphery—low use

Planting area—low use

Seating area—high use

House

LIGHT SHADE
Periphery—low use

Driveway

FULL SUN
Lawn—high use

FULL SUN
Planting area—low use

FULL SUN
Slope—low use

FULL SUN
Slope—low use

Simplicity in Design

Betty Ajay practices what she preaches. A landscape architect, she encourages the use of large masses of low-maintenance evergreen ground covers—especially in places where they can soften the heaviness of paving materials like stone and brick. It's an approach that results in clean, simple lines and reduced yard work. That's what you'll find at her Connecticut home as well as the homes of many of her clients.

For lots generous in size, lawn is the quickest and easiest way to cover ground where the natural vegetation has been removed. But Betty has significantly reduced the size of her lawn by planting large expanses of evergreen pachysandra and masses of low-growing hollies, and by creating large buffers of trees along the property's periphery. Although leaves must be raked out in the fall, the pachysandra requires little or no upkeep, and the shrubs only need occasional trimming.

The simplicity of Betty's approach to ground covers suits the clean lines of her house well. So does her front terrace, which spans the length of the main house. The gray flagstone blends naturally with the gray siding, and built-in planters filled with dwarf hollies offer an innovative alternative to railing—which would have significantly altered the look of the house. Wide, curving stone steps are edged in cobbles, also providing a comfortable approach to the house.

▲**Lawn and pachysandra** are the most prominent ground covers on this property. The curving edge of the pachysandra follows the gentle contours of the land.

▲ **A wide terrace and broad steps** balance the house shape and size. Planting beds were built into the terrace for shrubs, which (on low terraces only) eliminate the need for railings.

▶ **Low shrub masses** are also used effectively as ground cover. These hollies have a naturally attractive horizontal habit that requires only occasional shaping.

◀Hostas, though not ever-green, make an excellent massed ground cover in shade. The bold foliage becomes a nice contrast to lawn.

▼If you have a large expanse of lawn, consider breaking it up with island beds or small groves of trees to reduce routine chores like mowing. Planting slopes with low-maintenance ground covers is another good option.

climates. Consult your local nursery for the best plants for your climate, or choose from nonliving ground covers.

- **Sunlight**—Most lawns require full sun for healthy growth. Alternative ground covers are available for all kinds of light conditions.
- **Activities**—How you use a space, or even whether you use a space, has bearing on your choice of ground cover.
- **Soil conditions**—Before you make your selection, assess whether your soil is wet or dry, alkaline or acidic, and mostly clay, sand, or loam.
- **Maintenance**—Lawn is very high maintenance; most alternative ground covers require very little ongoing maintenance.
- **Budget**—Lawns are the least expensive ground cover to install but most expensive to maintain. Paved surfaces are just the opposite—expensive to install but with little or no ongoing maintenance costs. Mulches and evergreen ground covers fall somewhere in between.

Lawns

▲ Edging laid flush with the lawn plays three roles in the garden: It gives the lawn a clean, crisp edge; keeps grass out of the perennial borders; and makes mowing easier. In this garden, a second, upright edging adds an ornamental touch.

The sun-drenched view across an open lawn, especially in late spring and early summer, when lawns are at their best, is enchanting. Yet those that look best are not the endless lawns but those with definition: a broad, curving sweep of green set against a sunny border; a circle of lawn interrupted by the strong lines of a path or terrace; a rectangular patch surrounded by a picket fence; a wide, green path gently curving through a series of island beds. The secret to making a bigger impact with your lawn is making it smaller and more distinctive.

Especially nice are strong, voluptuous curves. Avoid making small, wiggly curves that are dwarfed by the immensity of the outdoors; what you want are deep dips and broad curves. Stretch out a sun-warmed garden hose to experiment with the lines. Run your lawn mower along those lines. If they are fun to follow, you've done a good job. If it's

Choosing the Right Grass

When it comes to grasses, some like it hot, and others do not—so your first challenge is selecting a grass suitable to your climate. Cool-season grasses like bluegrasses (*Poa* spp.), perennial ryegrass (*Lolium perenne*), bents (*Agrostis* spp.), and fescues (*Festuca* spp.) grow throughout most of North America and are frequently sown as blends of several grass species for greater disease resistance. They thrive in moist, cool climates and will brown out during hot summer droughts if not watered. Fescues are the most cold tolerant, braving the cold winters of USDA Hardiness Zone 2.

Warm-season grasses like zoysia (*Zoysia* spp.), Bermuda (*Cynodon dactylon*), and St. Augustine (*Stenotaphrum secundatum*) are better suited to hot climates like Florida and southern California. St. Augustine grass is the most heat tolerant, growing happily even in Zone 10. Warm-season grasses grow in more moderate climates but will turn brown in cool weather. Because most warm-season grasses are creepers and do not mix well, they are typically sown as a single species.

Light conditions will also play a role in the grass you select. Most grasses prefer full sun, but some will toler-

▲ This lawn has a very definite curving shape complemented by gently rolling berms, or mounds. They give a front yard a sculpted feeling that is pleasing to the eye but may make it less suitable for games and activities.

ate moderate shade. Among cool-season grasses, look to the fescues. Chewings fescue (*Festuca rubra* var. *commutata*) and creeping red fescue (*Festuca rubra* var. *rubra*) are the most shade and drought tolerant. Some varieties of Kentucky bluegrass (*Poa pratensis*) are also shade tolerant. For warm-season grasses, St. Augustine grass is your best bet; it creates a dense turf in shaded landscapes. Bahia grass (*Paspalum notatum*) is also a good shade-tolerant choice for hot climates.

tough to cut, you've made the curves too tight. Geometric lawns work too, particularly in a formal landscape or a small, enclosed yard. If you've got a small patch of flat lawn, a square, rectangle, or other distinct shape might work best. If your lawn abuts a natural area, such as a meadow or woodland, a gentle curve is more appropriate for the border. Set the mower blade higher or mow this area less often to create a subtle transition.

To keep your lawn edges neat in refined areas, install a mowing strip. A border of brick, cobbles, or other material

Seed or Sod?

Lawn grasses are most often purchased as seed or sod—though not all grasses are sold in both forms. In fact, most mixed-species lawns are only available as seed. Which method you use for installation depends on availability, your needs, and your budget. Seeding is the least expensive method of installation and can be used to create a well-adapted, deep-rooted lawn. However, it may take up to a year for a seeded lawn to become firmly established, and you'll need to be diligent about weeding and watering during that year. Sod is considerably more expensive (costing up to 10 times more than seed) but can create a lush lawn the day it is installed and only needs a few weeks to establish roots. Sod is an excellent choice for small, formal patches of lawn in a front yard, while larger expanses are usually seeded.

will keep the grass in the lawn and any plantings in their place and, at the same time, simplify mowing. The mowing will go faster, and you'll rarely need to haul out the hand shears, weed trimmer, or edging tool. Though a 4-inch border will do, a more generous 10-inch border will allow lush perennials to spill out from the beds without getting nipped by a mower, and edging closer to 2 feet wide can double as a garden path. The key to installing edging is placing the material flush with the ground so the lawnmower wheel will run over it easily and cut all your grass at the same height.

There are many grasses to choose from, so don't just grab the first bag of seed you see at the nursery. Because grasses vary in durability and appearance, be sure to match the grass to your needs. For a small, formal lawn where appearance is important, you'll probably want to stick with a single species for its uniform appearance. Perennial ryegrass, red fescue, Kentucky bluegrass, Bermuda grass, and zoysia are all good choices. Though they look good, these grasses can't take heavy traffic and are more susceptible to disease. For high-impact areas where durability is more important than

▲ **Small lawns can make a big impression.** This lawn, just large enough for a game of croquet, sets off the perennial border beautifully.

good looks, choose among mixtures of perennial ryegrass and tall fescues for cool climates, and cultivars of St. Augustine grass for warm climates. These lawns won't look as uniform, but if you mix tough grasses, they should be able to stand much more wear and tear. An ecological option is to choose from seed mixes that include small herbaceous plants such as clover. Upon close inspection, they may look a little ragged, but they should adapt more readily to your conditions and provide a solid, sturdy ground cover.

When you're designing a lawn, it also pays to think about your watering needs and resources—especially if you live in a drought-prone area. Between erratic weather patterns and extensive development in so many cities, water rationing has become commonplace throughout much of the country—not just in the arid Southwest. For these reasons, it's a good idea to choose a drought-tolerant grass no matter where you live. Many of the fescues, in particular, have deep roots that seek out moisture in the soil and don't need to be watered as often.

▼ **Curved lawns look very natural.** Go for deep dips and broad curves, not wiggly little lines. Flat lawns like this one are ideal for children's games.

Alternative Ground Covers

▲ **This gardener has planted a variety** of ground covers in her yard. In addition to a central lawn and perennial beds, you'll find masses of ivy, mondo grass, blue-eyed grass, and pachysandra.

While lawns are the traditional ground cover favored throughout much of the country, more and more homeowners are discovering the benefits of alternative ground covers. Though they may cost more to install, they are much less expensive and considerably less time consuming to maintain. Planted in a mass, they create an evergreen canvas not all that different from grass when viewed from a distance. Because there are more varieties to choose from, they can be adapted to any site. And though most can't be walked on, you can create paths through them. Many have the added benefit of seasonal interest—with flowers, berries, or colorful foliage.

Many different types of plants are suitable to serve as ground covers. Depending on whether you want a uniform look or more of a tapestry, you may plant a single large mass of one ground cover, or smaller masses of several different ground covers. Your plantings can be a smooth, consistent texture, or a painterly composition of plants with different heights, colors, forms, and textures. Here are some of the different groups of plants to consider as massed ground covers:

• **Runners**—These plants spread by an extensive network of aboveground or underground runners. *Pachysandra terminalis*, which sends up new shoots and foliage from the root system, is a good example; many ferns also spread this way. Ivy (*Hedera* spp.) and periwinkle (*Vinca minor*) are both aboveground runners. If you brush the foliage aside, you will see the long stems and notice that they are sending out roots.

Evergreen Ground Covers

PROSTRATE

Cliff green	*Paxistima canbyi*
Creeping lilyturf	*Liriope spicata*
Japanese spurge	*Pachysandra terminalis*
Lesser periwinkle	*Vinca minor*
Mondo grass	*Ophiopogon japonicus*
Prostrate rosemary	*Rosmarinous officinalis* 'Irene'
Sargent juniper	*Juniperus sargentii* 'Glauca'
Snow in summer	*Cerastium tomentosum*
Sun rose	*Helianthemum nummularium*
Sweet violet	*Viola odorata*
Taiwan bramble	*Rubus pentalobus*
Wall germander	*Teucrium chamaedrys* 'Prostratum'

◄Lilyturf

LOW GROWING (1 TO 2 FEET)

Blue Carpet juniper	*Juniperus squamata* 'Blue Carpet'
Creeping St. John's wort	*Hypericum calycinum*
Dwarf heavenly bamboo	*Nandina domestica* 'Harbor Dwarf'
Greater periwinkle	*Vinca major*
Heath	*Erica carnea*
Large blue fescue	*Festuca amethystina* 'Superba'
Point Reyes creeper	*Ceanothus gloriosus*
Sedges	*Carex* spp.
Sweet box	*Sarcococca hookeriana* var. *humilus*
Wintercreeper	*Euonymous fortunei*

MEDIUM HEIGHT (2 TO 3 FEET)

Australian Bluebell	*Sollya heterophylla*
Chinese juniper	*Juniperus chinensis* 'Saybrook Gold'
English lavender	*Lavandula angustifolia*
English yew	*Taxus baccata* 'Repandens'
French lavender	*Lavandula stoechas*
Leatherleaf sedge	*Carex buchananii*
Pheasant's tail grass	*Stipa arundinaceae*

- **Creepers**—These are slower-growing spreaders, such as thyme (*Thymus* spp.) and baby's tears (*Soleirolia soleirolii*), which create dense mats when they spread. They are good for smaller spaces and for filling in cracks between pavers.
- **Horizontal shrubs**—The best-known ground cover in this category is probably creeping juniper (*Juniperus horizontal-*

is), though creeping rosemary is also an excellent choice in moderate climates.

- **Clumping perennials**—Many low-growing perennials multiply rapidly and make a nice thick ground cover in just a few years. Daylilies (*Hemerocalis* spp.) are often used for this purpose.
- **Ornamental grasses and grass-like plants**—This is one of the broadest categories of ground covers. In addition to small grasses, there are sedges and grassy-looking plants like lilyturf (*Liriope* spp.) and pinks (*Dianthus* spp.).
- **Small, mounding shrubs**—Many shrubs make wonderful ground covers when planted in masses. Azaleas (*Rhododendron* spp.) are often planted this way in the South. Heaths (*Erica* spp.) and ground-cover roses (*Rosa* spp.) are good choices in other regions.

If your front yard is dominated by large hardwoods, it won't take long to discover that it's next to impossible to get grass to grow there and very difficult to plant anything large

▲ **Most daylilies flower for only a few weeks** in summer, but the strappy foliage makes an attractive ground cover for many months. Though not evergreen, daylilies do an admirable job of controlling erosion, even in winter.

▶ **Several types of shrubs can** be massed to create a tapestry-like ground cover. In most cases, you'll want to choose from shrubs that grow to 1 to 3 feet tall. Along the edges of your property, you may prefer something a little larger.

A Natural Collaboration

The lawn simply didn't work. According to landscape architect John Harper, the lawn in Dean Bates's and Shirl Handley's front yard "served no particular function, turned brown and patchy every summer, required frequent fertilization, and had to be reseeded each fall." Typical of those of many older Southern homes, this front lawn was competing with the substantial root system and shady canopy of a large old oak. And the oak was winning on all counts.

Though they presented a challenge to the lawn, the conditions created by the oak were ideal for the native wildflowers that bloom each spring throughout northern Georgia, and the ferns and shrubs that leaf out following the spring show. So rather than fight nature, John decided to work with it by planting native wildflowers and shrubs that change from season to season. And though it's the only lawnless front yard on the street, it looks perfectly natural because it blends in with the surrounding woodlands that fill many side yards and back yards.

In addition to filling the front yard with native plants, John also widened the nar-

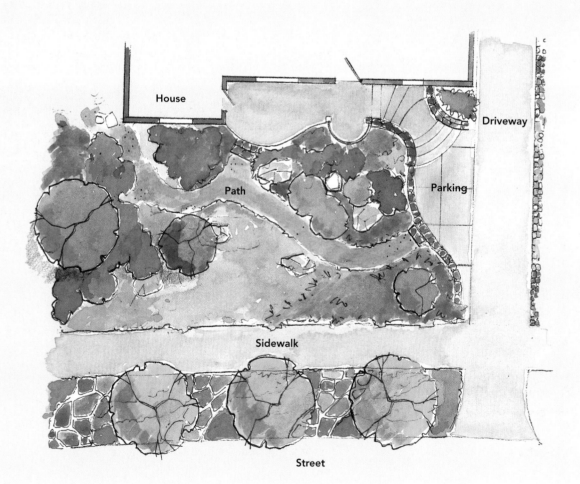

◄This no-lawn landscape draws its inspiration from nature. In place of evergreen masses, plantings are diversified and include mostly natives. It's an approach that works exceedingly well beneath huge old shade trees.

▼Before the landscape renovation, the entry was much smaller; maintaining a good-looking lawn was a constant battle.

row driveway with stone cobbles and redesigned the front entry (when they discovered the front porch was dilapidated). This new entry is much more inviting and accessible than the old one. It features curving stacked-stone walls, broad flagstone steps, custom wrought-iron railings, and built-in path lighting.

beneath many trees. Some homeowners choose to let nature provide its own ground cover and simply thin out plants that become too weedy. Another approach is to plant native species especially suited to these conditions and allow them to spread at their own pace. Though you might cover this area with a mass of plants, such as spreading ferns, it is often easier and more natural looking to plant a mix of under-story trees, shrubs, and perennial ground covers. Plantings here will be slower to take root and spread but can be surrounded with mulch, which will look nice and help keep the weeds down.

Nonliving Ground Covers

Not all ground has to be covered with plants—whether lawns, evergreen ground covers, or garden plants. In fact, some of the most functional spaces in the front yard are paved—paths, driveways, parking, terraces, patios, and courtyards. These last three, in particular, are excellent ways to make use of your front yard and reduce the size of your lawn. But since both paving materials and seating areas have been covered extensively in other chapters, we'll focus here on two other commonly used nonliving ground covers: gravel and mulch.

In hot, arid regions of the country, where extensive use of lawns or evergreen ground covers is impractical, finely chipped gravel is often the ground cover of choice. It keeps the soil cooler and helps to retain the little moisture there even in the heat of summer. Many drought-tolerant plants like cacti, succulents, and desert wildflowers enjoy growing

▼ **In spaces that are hard to mow** or that could be used for activities, paving is an alternative ground cover. Though it is often an excellent choice, keep in mind that paving increases the flow of runoff into drainage systems while it reduces the amount of water absorbed by the soil for plants.

◀In hot, dry climates that can't easily support lawns or other lush ground covers, finely chipped gravel is among the best ground covers. It allows the little water that falls to reach the soil, native wild-flowers and succulents can be planted directly through it, and it blends in with the surrounding natural environment.

in ground covered in a light layer of chipped gravel. It does not break down, so except for the gravel that gets kicked up over the years, it shouldn't have to be replaced or replenished. It comes in a variety of hues, from brown and buff to gray and terra-cotta, so it can be coordinated with your home and surrounding landscape.

Another nonliving ground cover is mulch. Technically, most mulch was once living, but whether pine needles, ground bark, or cocoa hulls, it has reached a point of decay. And that's precisely why mulch makes a good ground cover. It is a natural material, so it blends into the landscape almost seamlessly. And as it slowly breaks down, it nourishes the soil beneath. The only drawback is that it has to be replaced periodically. Because pine straw breaks down easily, you may need to spread fresh bales each spring or fall. A thick layer of hardwood mulch or bark chips, however, may only need to be replenished every few years.

Mulches make good transitional ground covers. If you have an area you'd eventually like to plant, simply cover it with mulch until you have the time and money for the

▲Pine needles are another good ground-cover mulch. They spread easily and mat down quickly for a clean, smooth surface. Here, they help control erosion on this bank while the ivy gets established.

Ground-Cover Mulches

Mulches vary from one part of the country to another based on what can be most easily and affordably attained. Of course, not all mulches used in the garden are suitable for use as front-yard ground covers. Wheat straw, for instance, is great for a vegetable garden but looks messy as a ground cover. The following mulches are commonly available and make excellent ground covers:

Cocoa bean hulls—A dark, attractive mulch that smells a bit like chocolate when stepped on.

Hardwood mulches—The bark and clippings of different kinds of hardwood trees are ground or shredded into easily spreadable mulch. They vary in color, fragrance, and consistency. Because hardwood mulch causes nitrogen to be tied up temporarily, you may need to add some nitrogen to the soil if you plant in this area.

Pine straw—Needles from pine trees, most readily available in the South, are raked and sold by the bale.

Pine bark—Sold as nuggets or mini-nuggets, depending on the size of the chips, and chosen based on their appearance. The nuggets are larger and coarser; the mini-nuggets, a bit more refined, break down faster.

▲**Mulches can cover patches of ground.** They are especially useful in areas designated for mixed beds or other ground covers that won't be planted for a year or two. The ground bark in this landscape provides a low-cost, low-maintenance ground cover. As it breaks down, it will enrich the soil below.

project. By then, the soil will be enriched and easy to plant. (Conversely, if you had planted the area in grass, you'd have to remove the sod and amend the soil.) If your space is small, you can buy mulch by the bag or bale at any garden center, nursery, or home center. If you're planning to cover a larger area, consider buying it by the truckload. As long as you can back the truck up near the area to be mulched, it's quicker and easier to spread in bulk, it costs less, and you're not left with lots of plastic bags to place in the trash.

8

Plantings

▶Trailing rosemary cascades over a retaining wall beneath a steep slope.

ront yards need not be limited to lawns, foundation beds, and hedges. They are also ideal places for beds, borders, and woodland groves. Such mixed plantings can be placed beside paths and driveways or along the periphery, or they may dominate your front yard. Plantings can be as simple as a few annuals planted beneath a lamppost, or as elaborate as a fenced cottage garden. Mixed plantings with evergreen trees and shrubs can be placed to screen views or buffer wind. A woodland grove is a wonderful low-maintenance way to reduce the size of your lawn and create a habitat for small wildlife. Perennial borders planted against a fence or evergreen hedge will add a splash of color throughout the growing season. And a series of gently curving island beds can transform your front yard into a strolling garden.

Front yards of all shapes and sizes are suitable for plantings. The types you choose will be determined by the style of your house, what is considered acceptable in your neighborhood, your native environment, and how much time you wish to spend tending the plantings. While some need very little care after planting, others require regular attention—especially during the growing season.

◀Island beds with gracefully curving edges float in a sea of lawn. They can be filled with small trees, shrubs, perennials, annuals, and bulbs.

In fact, ongoing care for plantings is much more important in a front yard than in a back yard. While we might "let things go" a little in the back yard when we travel or get busy with other activities, it's best to keep a front yard looking reasonably neat at all times. In winter, when you may not spend time in your back yard, you still come and go daily through your front yard, and it remains on view for your neighbors. So think carefully about the maintenance requirements of the plants you select, as well as their seasons of interest. Disease-resistant, repeat-blooming landscape roses that need little pruning, for instance, make much more sense than leggy, disease-prone Hybrid Tea roses that bloom for only a short period of time—no matter how beautiful their blossoms. And while fast-growing trees such as Bradford pear (*Pyrus calleryana* 'Bradford') and Leyland cypress (x *Cupressocyparis leylandii*) may make an impact in the landscape in only a few years, they tend to have weak wood that may snap under the weight of snow and ice or in high winds.

▲ This pocket planting of ferns, ivies, and geraniums has long-season good looks. Except for occasional watering and the removal of spent flowers, it requires little care.

◄**Retaining walls make** excellent backdrops for borders and offer a creative solution for steep yards. This one includes several levels and puts plants at eye level.

►**Herbs and grasses are low-maintenance plantings;** once established, they should need little supplemental water in most climates. Grasses should be cut back once a year—usually in early spring before they begin putting out new growth. Some herbs appreciate a little light pruning from time to time, which promotes bushy growth.

Drip for Dry Spells

Ideally, the plants we place in a garden should be able to survive on natural rainfall. But most new plantings need a full growing season to become established—especially if they are planted in spring or summer—and long periods of drought will stress even the toughest of plants. Drip irrigation systems are the most efficient way to meet a garden's supplementary watering needs. They should be designed and installed when you create your beds, before the plants go in.

Drip system technology has improved greatly over the past decade. Emitters last longer, hoses are more resistant to wear and tear, and sensors can now detect soil moisture levels so the systems turn on only when needed (which is important considering how taxed many municipal water systems are due to burgeoning growth). A simple drip system can be easily attached to a hose bib and installed in an afternoon. No glue is required—just screw, push, or snap the parts together like tinker toys. You can run feeder lines to individual plants, or use evenly spaced emitter lines to spread the water throughout a bed.

Clean Lines Complement a Craftsman Home

David Ketchum loves to garden but wanted some help redesigning the front yard to suit his recently renovated Craftsman home. Because the house had such strong lines, similarly strong lines were needed in the yard. We started by giving the lawn a distinct shape and well-defined edging—a bluestone mowing strip wide enough to double as a path in wet weather. The lawn is slightly domed in the middle for drainage and looks like an emerald cushion, begging to be sat or walked upon. The driveways and paths were edged with brick, which widened them, toned down the concrete, and added color to the hardscape.

▲ A small but well-defined and neatly manicured lawn sets off planting beds. Container plantings accent the entry.

◀ Planting beds were placed around the periphery and in the sidewalk strip. The plantings are fairly low, so neighbors get a sense of passing through a garden when they walk down the street.

◀Random pieces of blue-stone create a wide edging that doubles as a narrow garden path when the grass is wet.

We created a plant palette to complement the pale, moss-green stucco walls—including wine-foliaged barberries, a light-green 'Sango-kaku' Japanese maple, and the evergreen, orange-brown pheasant's tail grass as foundation plants. Chartreuse-foliaged hostas and creeping jenny add a bright note, and purple-flowered rhododendrons, bellflowers, 'Salome' daffodils, and asters offer varied color through the seasons. The beds surrounding the yard were planted in layers—from low-growing ground covers to small, ornamental trees—to take advantage of the limited space and to better tie the house to the land.

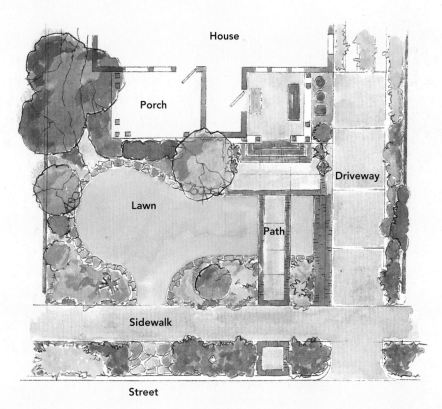

House

Porch

Lawn

Driveway

Path

Sidewalk

Street

Beds and Borders

Island beds and borders are the highlight of any garden. Though beds and borders may contain the same plants, the way they are viewed and therefore designed differs considerably. Borders are most often long and narrow, with a wall, fence, or hedge as a backdrop. Steep slopes, where retaining walls are used to create flat terraces, are also excellent places for borders. In contrast, island beds are freestanding—sometimes geometric in design, other times more naturalistic, with graceful curves. They can be placed just about anywhere in the yard—floating in the lawn, surrounding a mailbox or lamppost, along the periphery, or near a path, terrace, or driveway. Borders are viewed principally from the front, while island beds are visible from all sides. Even if a planting borders a driveway or path, it should be designed as an island bed since it doesn't have a solid backdrop.

▲ **Island beds, even if they border a driveway,** should be designed for view from all sides. This one has an asymmetric arrangement anchored by a dwarf pine.

◄ **A border has a backdrop,** and a fence serves admirably in that role. Make your beds 2 to 4 feet deep so you can include a variety of plants but can still reach to the back to deadhead spent flowers.

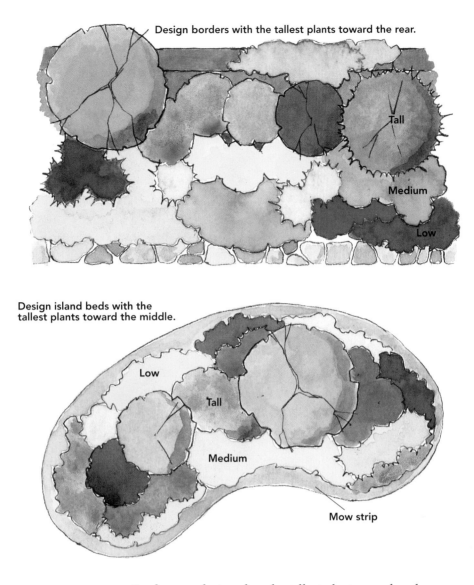

Design borders with the tallest plants toward the rear.

Tall

Medium

Low

Design island beds with the tallest plants toward the middle.

Low

Tall

Medium

Mow strip

Borders are designed so the tallest plants are placed toward the back, the shortest are in the front along the edge (and along the sides, if they are exposed), and the mid-height plants fill in the middle. This allows you to see all the plants and ensures that they receive adequate sunlight. But follow this rule loosely, as you don't want your border to look as ordered as a school picture. One way to break the routine is to place tall "see-through" plants toward the front of your border to create a veil of foliage or flowers through which you can see the rest of the garden. The tall *Verbena bonariensis*, which holds small clusters of purple blossoms high on erect stems, is a good example. So are many ornamental grasses.

Island beds, because they are viewed differently and do not have a backdrop, are usually designed with the tallest

Long-blooming Perennials

Black-eyed Susans	*Rudbeckia fulgida*
Bloody cranesbill	*Geranium sanguineum*
Catmint	*Nepeta x faassenii*
Indigo spires salvia	*Salvia pratensis* 'Indigo Spires'
Joe Pye weed	*Eupatorium fistulosum* 'Gateway'
Lenten rose	*Helleborus orientalis*
Mexican tarragon	*Tagetes lucida*
Pineapple sage	*Salvia elegans* 'Scarlet Pineapple'
Purple coneflower	*Echinacea purpurea*
Rose vervain	*Verbena* 'Homestead Purple'
Russian sage	*Perovskia atriplicifolia*
Shrub verbena	*Lantana camara* cultivars
Speedwell	*Veronica* 'Sunny Border Blue'
Spurge	*Euphorbia characias* ssp. *wulfenii*
Stella de Oro daylilies	*Hemerocallis* 'Stella de Oro'
Stonecrop	*Sedum* 'Herbsfreude'
Tickseed	*Coreopsis* 'Moonbeam'

▲Russian sage and purple coneflower

plants toward the middle, the smallest along the edge, and the medium-sized filler plants in between. In most cases, the tallest plants should not be placed dead center but slightly off-center or more toward one end of the border. If you have an irregularly shaped, curving border, place the tallest plant toward the wider end and work your design out from that starting point. To use an island bed as screening near the street or along a property boundary, you can create a berm—or mounded planting bed—in which to place the plants. This will raise the plantings an extra foot or two. Berms are also a good alternative if you have unusually difficult soil, as you don't have to dig as deep to amend the existing soil.

Beyond these basic design approaches, island beds and borders are otherwise very much alike. Both need to be narrow enough so you can reach into them to deadhead, prune, and tend plants (about 4 feet for a border and 8 feet for an island bed), or else they should include narrow stepping-

▲Borders, whether curving or straight, look nice around the periphery and edged with lawn. This one is layered in a naturalistic style—from canopy and understory trees to flowering shrubs and an assortment of perennials with contrasting foliage.

▲ **This front-yard garden includes a mix of** clumping evergreens, upright bulbs, bold-foliaged annuals, and long-flowering perennials for a scene that changes through the seasons.

▲ **The yellow flowers of Jerusalem artichoke are echoed** in the yellow-variegated foliage of nearby plants.

stone or mulch paths to keep you from stepping on plants or compacting the soil. If placed near the street, beds usually look best set back about 5 or 6 feet—both for better viewing and for safety when tending.

You can anchor beds and borders with shrubs or small, ornamental trees; add clusters of perennials; accent them with seasonal bulbs; and fill in any gaps with annuals (especially during the first few years, before the larger plants have reached full size). Keep in mind that flowers can be fleeting, so plants should be selected as much for their form and foliage as their blossoms (if not more so). And for those flowers, repeat bloomers or plants with a long season of bloom—six to eight weeks instead of just a few days—should play a leading role in the garden. For year-round interest, consider including some evergreens in your beds and borders. In regions with long winters, you may even want evergreens to dominate your plantings.

Seasonal changes make a garden more interesting and help you attune yourself to the cycles of life. Use a mix of plants to make a splash at different times of the year. Celebrate the arrival of spring with ferns that unfurl gracefully and bulbs that won't be deterred by a late-season cold snap. Usher in summer with a burst of flowers and bold, colorful foliage. Settle into fall with muted grasses, perennials with interesting seed heads, and shrubs with colorful stems or peeling bark. For the stillness of winter, select shrubs with bright berries or ornamental trees with graceful branching patterns.

Though entire books have been written about the art of planting design, the basics are really quite simple. All plants have shape, size, leaf form, texture, and color. Within any garden setting, you can make individual plants stand out by contrasting those elements. And you can make the individuals work together as a whole by repeating those elements. For instance, try placing smooth leaves next to coarse or

◀ Eye-catching plant combinations are a living art form, and creating contrast is one of the secrets to creating successful compositions. Contrast plant shapes, leaf sizes, and foliage and flower colors for a striking effect—and then repeat those same shapes, colors, and forms throughout the garden for a sense of unity.

▼ Select foliage and flower colors that complement the architectural elements of your home. Here, the owner chose a maple and New Zealand flax to harmonize with a lavender-purple courtyard wall.

hairy ones; large-leaved plants next to those with delicate or finely-cut foliage; tall, upright plants next to low, mounding ones; purple flowers next to yellow ones; burgundy foliage next to chartreuse foliage. But in doing so, repeat the individual plants, shapes, sizes, colors, or combinations throughout your bed or border for continuity. Clustering plants in small masses—say three, five, or seven of the same plant—also works and is easier to maintain. You can repeat the masses throughout the bed for unity.

Color is the most complex of the design elements. In addition to creating contrast with colors, you can achieve color harmonies by combining flowers that are very similar in hue. For instance, flowers in different shades of purple and pink are lovely together and create a soothing atmosphere. When designing color harmonies, contrasting colors (used with restraint) can provide an occasional accent in the garden. To purple and pink you might add a splash of yellow. Color schemes can also be based on the degree of color saturation—selecting a base color that runs the gamut from pastel to electric. And finally, white, gray-green, and silver are considered blending colors—they go with almost any

Plants with Striking Foliage

▲ Hosta, zonal geranium, and fern

Adam's needle	*Yucca filamentosa*
Bowles' golden sedge	*Carex elata* 'Aurea'
Bronze fennel	*Foeniculum vulgare*
Cardoon	*Cynara cardunculus*
Century plant	*Agave americana*
Coralbells	*Heuchera micrantha* var. *diversifolia* 'Palace Purple'
Ethiopian banana	*Ensete ventricosum*
Gunnera	*Gunnera manicata*
Indian shot	*Canna* 'Tropicana'
New Zealand flax	*Phormium tenax*
Purple sage	*Salvia officinalis* 'Purpurascens'
Rodgersia	*Rodgersia podophylla*
Sea holly	*Eryngium giganteum*
Smokebush	*Cotinus coggygria* 'Royal Purple'
Southern catalpa	*Catalpa bignonioides* 'Aurea'
Spurge	*Euphorbia characias* ssp. *wulfenii*

colors and make nice transitions if you are shifting your color scheme slightly from one section of the border to another. That said, you should use white with restraint in a colored garden, as white draws the eye more readily than any color and will quickly dominate your planting.

When evaluating color schemes, start by taking a look at your house. If it has painted details such as shutters, doors, or trim, or even distinctively colored brick, stone, or stucco, make sure your planting scheme complements these colors. If that's not an issue, then simply start with your favorite flower color and add a contrasting color, one or two harmonious colors, or different shades of that favorite color to create a color scheme.

Container Gardens

Container plantings look great flanking a front door, marking a path, or clustered in a courtyard. And if you do have beds and borders, you can use containers as a focal point or to fill a temporary gap.

There are many types of containers—pots of all shapes and sizes, square and rectangular box planters, window boxes, hanging baskets, and even recycled objects like buckets or crates. Like other garden ornaments, containers exist to suit the style of any garden. No matter what kind you choose, keep in mind that bigger is usually better. That's because large pots hold more soil and moisture and therefore need to be watered and fertilized less often. Of course, you can almost always find a perfect place for a small pot filled with a few succulents, and small pots can be moved around

▼Create garden vignettes with container plantings. This cluster of containers and ornaments highlights the side-yard entry.

more easily if weight is a concern. Make sure your pots have holes in the bottom and are filled with loose potting soil so they will drain easily. Consider placing feet or trays beneath your pots so they won't rot the wood or stain the concrete beneath them when water seeps out of the bottom.

The nice thing about container plantings is how easily they can be changed from season to season. Simply pull out the old plants and put in something new. If they were annuals, throw them on the compost pile. Just about any plant will grow in a pot—though plants with long taproots can be troublesome. Give them the same kind of light you would if you were growing them in the garden. Beneath a porch, you'll need shade plants. On an open, south-facing stoop or terrace, select sun-loving plants.

Container plantings are very versatile. You can grow just one plant in a pot or combine several plants in a single large pot. You can cluster several pots together in an asymmetric arrangement, line the steps leading to your door, or place matching container plantings on either side of a door. Combine plants the same way you would in the garden—contrasting plant shapes, sizes, leaf forms, colors, and textures for visual punch. If placing more than one plant in a pot, planter or window box, try positioning a distinctive plant with an upright habit toward the middle, a few trailing plants along the edges, and perhaps some mounding plants in between.

▲Big pots and architectural plants make a strong impression. In this case, the bold and colorful foliage draws your eye to the front door. Also, big pots don't have to be watered as often as small pots.

►Window boxes are an excellent way to bring plantings closer to eye level. Choose the largest box your window can support and fill it with a mix of upright, mounding, and trailing plants for best effect.

Cottage Gardens

A passion for gardening and a cottage, bungalow, or beach house are the ingredients for a cottage garden. Cottage gardeners tend to throw convention to the wind— eliminating lawns and foundation plantings, and replacing them with a plethora of plants and lots of personality.

First and foremost, a cottage garden is small. In addition, a cottage garden is generally characterized by a low enclosure— no more than 3 or 4 feet high—within which you'll find an abundance of flowers. Intersecting paths run through most cottage gardens, as much for access to all sides of planting beds as for circulation. Plantings run the gamut from herbs, vegetables, and flowers to native plants or even something a little more refined—such as sheared boxwood anchoring the

▼Cottage gardens are often surrounded by low fences and almost always contain a profusion of flowers. This gardener has a passion for Old Garden roses.

▲In this cottage garden, the emphasis is more on foliage than flower, but it still overflows with abundance. The widely spaced pickets give the garden an open, inviting look, while evergreen shrubs provide a dark background for interior plantings. Vines scramble up and over everything—the fence, arbor, and front entry.

corners of beds. Overall, however, the planting style is almost always loose and colorful, with lots of old-fashioned annuals and biennials like hollyhocks (*Alcea rosea*), foxgloves (*Digitalis purpurea*), and cosmos (*Cosmos bipinnatus*).

Beyond the prolific plantings, it's personalization that most characterizes cottage gardens. Though hardscaping is usually minimal, ornamentation is not. Chairs and benches, birdhouses and birdbaths, window boxes and colorful containers—even sculpture, found art, and folk art—are common elements. These ornamental elements reflect the architectural style of the house, regional aesthetics, and the personality of the homeowners. They are fun, eclectic, and often fanciful.

Most of the plants in cottage gardens are herbaceous, so they die back to the ground in winter. That's one of the reasons a low enclosure is important; it keeps the front yard looking good even in winter. A few evergreens, such as the boxwoods previously mentioned, along with evergreen herbs like rosemary (*Rosmarinus officinalis*), germander (*Teucrium chamaedrys*), and lavender (*Lavandula* spp.), can also add winter interest. And cool-weather annuals like pansies (*Viola* x *wittrockiana*) or vegetables such as kale, cabbage, or chard can be tucked in for a splash of color.

A Plantsman's Showcase

When Thomas Vetter bought his home, there was no garden, a concrete path stopped short of the street, and the house had little personality. What a difference a porch, some paint, and a gardener can make!

Over the years, Thomas has transformed an ordinary lot into a gardener's showcase—beautifully designed and with a stunning collection of plants. His design philosophy is

▲ **You can hardly tell it's the same place.** A portico, paint, new path, and plenty of plantings have completely transformed this front yard.

◄ **A master plantsman is at work in this garden,** combining plants for their year-round good looks. Yellow is the predominant color; burgundy and lavender are used for accent.

◀Decorative items
are common in cottage
gardens. This one serves
as a focal point in a
planting bed.

straightforward: "Pick plants that have good
structure and then include a mix of them
throughout the garden." He also places
more emphasis on a plant's foliage than its
flowers. And because he wants the garden
to look good year-round, he often tests
plants in pots for a year to see how they
perform before placing them in the ground.
From bare branches that catch the lightest
snow of winter to upright corymbs of flower
heads to flushes of golden foliage, this garden is eye-catching in every season.

He started by designing wide berms that
surround the yard and are filled with excellent soil for his plants. Only a small patch
of lawn remains, but it sets off his planting
beds nicely. He also removed the concrete
path and, instead, ran a path of bricks and
pavers from the driveway to the front door.
The concrete was recycled to create an artful path leading from the front yard,
through an arbor, to a side-yard garden.

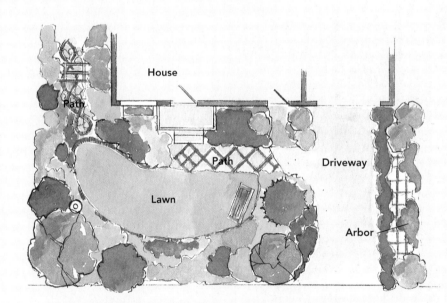

Woodland Groves

Trees are valued in the landscape for many reasons. Originally, they were planted in front yards to provide nuts and fruits. But as front yards have evolved from working areas to more ornamental spaces, their role has changed. Today, trees are more often planted for their sheer beauty, screening, and shade. Near windows, deciduous trees can offer shade in summer and allow sunlight in winter. Along your periphery, a cluster of evergreen trees can screen unwanted views, buffer wind or noise, and increase your sense of privacy. In mixed borders, they can enhance your garden in every season. And planted as a small grove or woodland,

▼A grove of canopy trees underplanted with azaleas and shade-tolerant perennials creates a nice woodland setting in this front yard. An alluring main path winds between the grove and house.

▲ **Tall evergreens provide dense screening** between neighbors, while a redbud offers an inviting overhead canopy for this bench. Redbuds flower in spring and display their flattened pods in summer.

they can create a natural, low-maintenance setting that attracts birds and other small wildlife.

Groves of trees are especially nice along the side and front periphery. A grouping of evergreens will form a dense screen, while deciduous trees create a loose, more open buffer. For a natural-looking stand, consider planting one or two species in a random manner—perhaps with trees of different sizes and ages. Slender, multitrunked trees such as birches (*Betula* spp.) are especially suited to small groves, and they are lovely surrounded by lawn or underplanted with an evergreen ground cover and spring bulbs. If you're planting along a property line, keep the ultimate spread of your trees in mind. In most places, your neighbors can cut any limbs that encroach their property—whether near the ground or hanging above. Road and utility crews also have the right to trim any trees within their right of way, so be

Trees for Shade and Beauty

Crape myrtle	*Lagerstroemia* spp.
Eastern redbud	*Cercis canadensis*
Fringe tree	*Chionanthus virginicus*
Honeylocust	*Gleditsia triacanthus* 'Sunburst'
Japanese snowbell	*Styrax japonicus*
Kousa dogwood	*Cornus kousa*
Olive	*Olea europaea*
Maidenhair tree	*Ginko biloba* 'Autumn Gold'
Palo verde	*Parkinsonia florida*
Paper-bark maple	*Acer griseum*
Queen palm	*Syagrus romazoffiana*
River birch	*Betula nigra* 'Heritage'
Saucer magnolia	*Magnolia* x *soulangeana*
Sourwood	*Oxydendrum arboreum*
Yoshino cherry	*Prunus* x *yedoensis*

▲Japanese snowbell

sure your trees won't hang out into the street or grow up into power, cable, or telephone lines.

Similarly, if planting shade trees close to your house—whether as a specimen planting in a bed or border or as a cluster of trees—think about the trees' mature size before digging your holes. You don't want outstretched limbs to brush against the siding or hang over the roof. In most cases, it's best for only the very edge of the tree canopy to reach the roof. Though it may not shade your roof, it will still shade your windows. Select trees with deep roots rather than shallow, spreading roots, and plant them a generous distance from your house foundation, driveway, and paths. And if you have a sewage drain field in your front yard, avoid planting any trees in this area—as the roots will penetrate and damage the drain pipes.

▲ **This allée of trees was recently planted** along a path leading from the front to side yards. It will grow to form a lovely canopy overhead and provide subtle screening between these two areas of the yard.

If you live in a region noted for its woodlands and have a moderate-sized to large front yard, consider leaving or establishing a natural woodland area. Unlike a grove, which has a slightly manicured look, woodlands are much more natural, with a mix of canopy trees, understory trees and shrubs, and small shrubs, perennials, and ground covers. If planted with mostly native species, this area will blend in with the surrounding natural landscape and more or less take care of itself over the years.

9

Lighting

▶**Lighting can create drama in the garden.** Here, the shadows are as eye-catching as the subject.

Most homes have porch lights and perhaps a lamppost along a path or floodlight near the garage. But landscape lighting can be so much more. It not only makes finding and approaching your house easier and safer after dark but can extend the hours you spend outdoors and create a warm, inviting environment.

Effective outdoor lighting is subtle, not bold. In most cases, less (or at least less intensive) is more. You need just enough light to move around safely—not enough to read a book or work at a computer. Unlike indoors, where you have walls to reflect and even out the light, bright lights can be harsh set against the night sky. When you light an area, you draw attention to it and away from other areas. For this reason, it's best not to light your entire yard.

The light intensity of individual fixtures will vary throughout the landscape depending on the distance between the light and the subject, the surface the light falls upon (dark surfaces absorb light, while light surfaces reflect light), the ambience you wish to create, and the relationship between the various lights in the landscape. The brightest lights should draw your eyes to

◀**Lighting serves multiple roles in the landscape. Recessed lights over the front entry are** functional; spotlights on the water feature create a dramatic focal point; subtle tea lights hung on the overhead canopy help create atmosphere.

▲Though the lights on these gateposts are principally functional, they are also artistic—echoing the grid used on the iron fence.

focal points in the landscape, while lower lights will create mood or meet basic safety needs.

There are two basic forms of landscape lighting: functional and accent. Functional lighting is just that—lighting that allows you to function safely in an area after dark. It includes lighting for paths and steps so you can traverse them safely, as well as for more general needs, such as illuminating entries, courtyards, parking courts, or terraces. The second type of lighting highlights architectural features of your home, garden ornaments, trees, and other special plantings. In other words, it is used to create mood rather than to help you do anything or go anywhere.

Turn the Lights Out

Studies have shown that plants, like people, perform their best if they get a good night's rest in complete darkness. So turn out the lights when you don't need them. It will save on your power bill, too.

The Scoop on DIY Kits

In recent years, many do-it-yourself outdoor lighting kits have been introduced. Most are reasonably easy to install and provide an affordable option for basic safety lighting needs, such as lighting a path or steps. However, the types and styles of fixtures are limited, their range (the distance they can be run from a house) is short, and their capacity is limited. Outdoor fixtures take a lot of abuse, and because of the way they are installed (both wires and fixtures are above ground), do-it-yourself fixtures and wiring are especially subject to wear and tear. And finally, even though these are low-voltage fixtures, they must still be handled with care. Bulbs can get hot enough to burn. If your needs are limited and you feel comfortable handling electrical projects, a lighting kit from a home center may be exactly what you need. For more durable or extensive lighting customized to your landscaping needs, consider contacting a lighting designer.

Rather than delving into watts, spots, and electrical engineering, we're going to look at landscape lighting from a general design viewpoint: what you can light, why you should light it, and, in general, what form of lighting best suits each situation. This way, you can better evaluate your needs and communicate them to a lighting professional.

Though landscape lighting can be installed in mature landscapes, the ideal time to tackle electrical jobs is when you're building your home, installing a new landscape, or renovating an existing one. That's because it often requires digging holes and trenches, and some of the most attractive and durable lighting fixtures are actually built into steps, paths, and walls (though there are alternatives as well). Even if it requires a little groundwork, lighting can dramatically change the look of your home after dark and is well worth the effort.

◄ **This wood-and-copper lantern marks** the driveway entrance and lights a sitting wall that is a favorite gathering place for neighbors in the evening.

►**Wall-mounted downlights showcase** a collection of neatly trimmed dwarf boxwoods in containers as well as shed light on this staircase. Because it is a whole flight of steps rather than just a few, multiple lights were required for adequate coverage.

Lighting Maintenance

Maintaining outdoor lights is a little more involved than maintaining most indoor lights. To begin with, the fixtures are exposed to the elements. Dirt and leaves get lodged in ground fixtures, and high winds (as well as arborists) can knock tree lights out of position. Many fixtures—like those hung in trees or hidden behind shrubs—are hard to reach when it's time to change them, which is recommended at least every two years. And replacement parts, including the lamps or bulbs, are not always easy to find. For this reason, you might wish to discuss an ongoing maintenance plan with your lighting designer. Consider having someone familiar with your landscape lighting inspect it at least annually to replace bulbs, adjust fixtures, and repair any damaged parts.

Lighting Paths, Steps, and Driveways

▼On small lots, a lamppost is often all that is needed to light the way. This one doubles as a support for a climbing rose.

The most important role of lighting is that of safety, and your top priority should be lighting paths and steps. This includes the steps leading down from your porch or stoop; the path and steps leading to the street, driveway, or parking court; and any other paths or steps used at night. Often we assume that porch lights or lampposts provide sufficient light on nearby steps, and sometimes they do. But remember that when you walk out your front door, you are most often going from a brightly lit area into darkness, and eyes need time to adjust. Extra lights on steps and along the path will help.

When lighting paths and steps, you want relatively even-spaced lights that shed their light down and out, not up. Because beams lose intensity the farther away they are from their source, it is important to overlap the beams of lights placed alongside a path to create an evenly lit surface. For a narrow path, lights along one side are usually sufficient. For paths wider than 4 feet, lights on both side will do a better job.

For steps, the best approach is to place lights at both the top and bottom of the flight, and on both sides—regardless of width. If the steps are long, you may need interim lights along the way as well. If there are only two or three steps, a single light with good beam spread placed next to the middle step may do, though two or more lights on steps are almost always preferable.

Though path lights—fixtures raised anywhere from a few inches to a foot or more on posts and designed to cast light down and out on a path—are the most common means of lighting paths and steps, they aren't the only option. Downlights placed high in trees are often used, especially if there is a broader area to be lit—such as a courtyard or surrounding plantings—though these should never be the sole lights for steps. And many fixtures can be built into retaining walls and steps—such as tread lights and sidelights—making

▲**Downlights hung in the arbor and in trees illuminate** steps and the courtyard. Lighting is also used to highlight garden sculpture.

▲ **Though driveway lights are rarely needed,** this one helps highlight where to turn into the drive from the street. It also helps those pulling in to avoid driving over plantings.

Beams should overlap slightly for even lighting on paths.

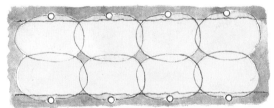

them much less obtrusive in the landscape, and somewhat less subject to wear and tear. You can even set filtered-glass blocks in a sidewalk and light them from below to gently illuminate the way.

Most driveway lights are more annoying than useful. Placing path lights along a driveway tends to make it look like an airstrip and will call attention to it, rather than to your house. Besides, you should be able to see just fine with the headlights on your car. There are times, however, when driveway lights make sense. If a driveway is unusually difficult to maneuver, perhaps because it is very narrow or has tight curves or because there is a steep drop-off along the shoulder, lighting can improve safety. And supplemental lighting helps in turnarounds, where you would be relying only on your car's backup lights, which are considerably dimmer than headlights. And finally, if your driveway doubles as the path to your front door for guests, some path lights will be appreciated.

Lighting Entries and Activity Areas

When you look at your front yard at night, the brightest area should be your front door. However, that doesn't mean it should be the harshest light. In fact, soft lights are the most pleasing—frosted bulbs and milky glass in fixtures are much easier on the eyes and create a warmer, more inviting mood. You can choose from overhead, recessed lights built into the porch ceiling or portico, hanging lanterns, or coach lamps placed on one or both sides of a door. Though spotlights placed in the yard to shine on an entry will certainly illuminate it, they tend to create glare, making it difficult for people to see, and so are best used to highlight other architectural features.

Activity zones like parking bays, courtyards, and terraces also need to be lit. In parking areas, soft lighting makes it easier to get in and out of a car, gather your belongings, and manage things like gifts or groceries. Traditional hardware-store floodlights are functional but offer little ambience. Instead, consider placing softer downlights in trees, on the garage, or against the house to illuminate a parking area. They can even be placed on automatic switches that sense the approach of a vehicle or person. Path lights, a lamppost, or lantern can mark the point where the path leads from the parking area to the door.

▲ Sconces or coach lamps can be placed on either side of a door or on the outside of a portico. This one is as attractive as it is useful and coordinates with the color of the shutters.

Enchanting After Dark

◄▲ **This fountain is lit principally from an overhead angle** for drama. It casts a deep shadow on the ground. Accent lighting draws attention to the fountain and vine-covered trellis, while downlights hung in trees provide even lighting on the terrace floor.

Mavin and Pete Howley live on a beautiful wooded lot beneath the graceful canopy of several large native California oaks. Without supplemental lighting, the entry to their home would indeed be very dark.

The entry garden, designed by Suzman Design Associates, includes a flagstone path that widens into a terrace, a shade garden, and a lovely tiered fountain that serves as the focal point of the entry. Lighting designer Anna Kondolf was called in to highlight these features so the garden could be enjoyed after dark.

Because it was a fairly complex project, she used a variety of lighting techniques. Downlights are hung in the trees for general illumination—to light the way from the parking area to the front door and in the terraced area. Some were placed to provide even illumination; others were installed above limbs to cast interesting shadows on the ground. Uplights were buried in the ground to highlight the dramatic branches of the oaks; spotlights were used to accent smaller ornamental trees and the fountain. And finally, path lights were used on side paths that run to the kitchen door and a side-yard garden. Together, these lights offer a whole new way of viewing the garden.

▲ **Uplighting highlights tree branches,** while downlighting through tree branches casts interesting shadows on the ground.

▲ **Both general and accent lighting** illuminate this deck, courtyard, and garden. Downlights hung from trees shed light on broad areas, while uplights call attention to the sculptural qualities of trees.

Courtyards and terraces may require more than one type of lighting. Most important is the general lighting, which again, can best be provided by downlights. However, you may also need some task lighting for a dining table, seating area, or barbecue grill. This too is most often supplied by downlights, but may be brighter or more directional. For a table, you might consider candles or perhaps an interesting lantern hanging from a tree limb or arbor. Accent lighting is also frequently used in courtyards or terraces.

Accent
Lighting

Accent lighting is the creative element of landscape lighting. It can be used to suggest mood or highlight focal points in the landscape. Focal points are often garden ornamentation such as sculpture, statuary, or water features, but they can be architectural features, such as stacked-stone walls or special plantings—perhaps a boxwood parterre or trees with interesting branching patterns. Though you want to emphasize these elements in the landscape, they should not be illuminated more brightly than your front door. In fact, accent lighting is often most effective when it is very subtle.

It is within this category of lighting that you will find the greatest variety of fixtures and lighting techniques. Floodlights can be used to "wash" a wall or object with light, often casting interesting shadows behind it. One effective technique is to "graze" a wall with light from an angle to emphasize its texture.

To highlight sculpture, statuary, fountains, or other ornamental objects, consider using several spotlights (which are more directional than floodlights). The number of lights you use and where you place them will vary the effect dramatically. A single light on a sculpture could create dramatic shadows; adding more lights would soften and reduce the shadows. If the sculpture is lit from behind, a silhouette would be created; if lit from the front, interesting shadows could be cast on a background wall; if lit from above, the shadows are cast on the ground; and if lit from all sides, shadows could be greatly reduced or eliminated.

▼ **Accent lighting calls attention to key plantings,** a water feature, a nicely detailed gate, a large sculptural pot, and metal sculptures of birds ready to take flight.

Uplight a tree by shining one or two spotlights into the branches.

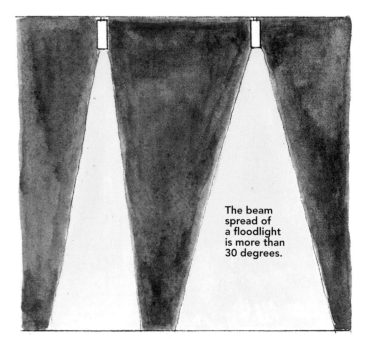

The beam spread of a floodlight is more than 30 degrees.

Uplights can be placed on or in the ground and directed up into trees to highlight their branches, which is especially effective with deciduous trees in winter. Downlights can be placed in trees to cast shadows of the branches on the ground. Installed near large, ornamental grasses, lights can emphasize subtle movements in the night garden.

Most water features look spectacular illuminated at night. Soft, general lighting will allow them to be seen while also blending them into the surrounding landscape. Spot lighting will call attention to water features and make them stand out. Waterproof lights inside a water feature are the most dramatic of all; they highlight the water itself.

In most cases, you want to see the object you are lighting and not the lights themselves. The exception would be specialty lights such candles, torches, and tea lights. Tea lights—tiny white lights on strings that can be hung along arbors, arches, eaves, and canopies, or wrapped around trees and shrubs—have become especially popular. They are similar to the lights we string up during the holidays but are made specifically for long-term outdoor use and can brighten a landscape any time of year.

Keep the Holidays Bright

Holiday lights are a booming business in America, and most of it falls into the do-it-yourself category with strings and swags of lights that can be hung from your house or wrapped around trees. As wonderful as these holiday lights are, most of the lights you buy at a drug or discount store can pose a fire hazard when left outdoors permanently. The wires and connections are not made to withstand the weather, and parts will rust from one holiday season to the next. Enjoy the season and then bring your lights in after the celebration is over. For a more permanent display, consider professional-grade tea lights designed for long-term outdoor wear and tear.

◀**Water can be illuminated in many ways**—from inside a water feature, for example, or by casting light upon the water feature. A spotlight shines toward the waterspout on this one, pulling out the rich color of the painted wall, highlighting the water as it splashes into the pool and calling attention to the sculptural figure overlooking the pool.

▲**This courtyard can be viewed** from the living room window. Cross-lighting on the dolphin water feature casts interesting shadows on the masonry wall behind.

▲**Some forms of lighting** are solely for drama, like this torch that highlights a recessed entry.

Credits

pp. ii–iii, 120, 126: Katherine Hoffman residence, Bethesda, MD; designed by Jeni Webber.

pp. 2, 84, 104–105: Bob McIntyre residence, Palo Alto, CA; designed by Jeni Webber.

pp. 3, 41, 79 (bottom), 88, 92 (top): Barbara and Gordon Robinson residence, Atlanta; designed by Paula Refi.

p. 4: Arlene Keene residence, Cumming, GA

p. 5: William R. Bechtold residence, Palo Alto, CA; designed by Louis J. Marano, Architect.

pp. 6, 112 (top): Louise Luthy residence, Seattle.

pp. 7, 156 (bottom): Scott Begnaud residence, Gainesville, GA.

pp. 8–9, 56 (bottom): Tim O'Hearn residence, Portland, OR; designed by Jeffrey Bale.

pp. 10, 33 (bottom left), 87, 137, 163 (top): David Ellis residence, Atlanta; designed by David Ellis & Brad McGill

pp. 11, 45 (right), 128: Paul & Heidi Morris residence, Seattle.

pp. 13 (top), 29: Karen Arcuri residence, Oakland, CA; painting by Christine Yang.

p. 13 (bottom): Harrison Petit residence, Portland, OR; designed by Jeffrey Bale.

pp. 14 (top), 47, 96–97, 103 (top), 143 (bottom): Seattle residence; designed by Keith Geller.

pp. 14 (bottom), 27, 28 (top), 160 (bottom): Rochelle Ford residence, Palo Alto, CA.

pp. 15, 71, 99 (bottom), 143 (top): Colonial Williamsburg.

pp. 16, 44: Diane & Bob Pagano residence, Lincoln, MA; designed by Maria von Brincken.

pp. 17, 48–49, 70 (top), 102, 133: Baltimore residence; designed by Mahan Rykiel Associates.

p. 18 (top): Lucy Hardiman residence, Portland, OR.

p. 18 (bottom): David Bennett McMullin residence, Atlanta.

pp. 19, 67, 83: Kevin Doyle residence, Dover, MA.

pp. 20, 66, 165 (top): Victor Vasquez residence, Phoenix; designed by Carrie Nimmer.

pp. 22–23: Carrie Nimmer residence, Phoenix.

pp. 25 (top), 36 (top), 99 (top), 162: Dan Cleveland & Jeffrey Rogerson residence, Atlanta; designed by Dan Cleveland.

p. 25 (bottom): Phoenix residence; designed by Carrie Nimmer.

pp. 26, 85 (right): Louise Poer residence, Atlanta.

p. 28 (bottom): Jack Bledsoe residence, Adamstown, MD.

pp. 30–31, 72, 177: Anna & Verne Davis residence, Atlanta; designed by Brooks Garcia.

pp. 32, 139: Barbara Blossom Ashmun residence, Portland, OR.

pp. 33 (top), 62 (top): Margaret de Haas van Dorsser residence, Portland, OR.

pp. 33 (bottom right), 61, 79 (top), 115 (top): Atlanta residence; designed by David Ellis & Brad McGill.

pp. 34, 74: Tim & Brooke Cohn residence, Oklahoma City; designed by Bill Renner.

p. 35: J.M. Solana residence, Savannah, GA

p. 36 (bottom): Richmond Hill Inn, Asheville, NC.

pp. 37, p. 39 (top), 152 (bottom): Ann & Eric Kastner residence, Palo Alto, CA; designed by Eric Kastner, Michael Agins & Barbara Yankow.

pp. 38, 98: Anne & Andy Sheldon residence, Atlanta.

p. 39 (bottom): Anne Reutinger residence, Oakland, CA; designed by Kirsten Berg.

pp. 40, 148 (top), 172, 185 (top): Paradise Valley, AZ, residence; designed by Steve Martino & Associates.

pp. 42–43, 95: Stephen & Meg Carruthers residence, Portland, OR; designed by Stephen J. Carruthers.

pp. 46 (top), 152 (top): Mary Li residence; Portland, OR; designed by Jeffrey Bale.

pp. 46 (bottom), 148 (bottom): James Simons residence, Atlanta.

pp. 50, 77 (top), 171: Weston, MA, residence; designed by Maria von Brincken.

p. 51 (top): David H. Jenkins residence, Atlanta, GA.

pp. 51 (bottom), 168: Millicent Zamirowski residence, Cumming, GA.

pp. 52, 115 (bottom), 123 (bottom), 136 (top): Janet Roberts residence, Portland, OR.

pp. 53, 150: Don & Patricia Ryan residence, Savannah, GA; designed by Ryan Garden Design.

pp. 54 (top), 60 (top): Sunaina & Peter Ruh residence, Palo Alto, CA; designed by Toni Heren with John Sousa.

pp. 54 (bottom), 141, 159 (top): Paula Refi residence, Atlanta.

p. 55 (top): Hugh & Joan Nichols residence, Savannah, GA.

pp. 55 (bottom), 159 (bottom), 161, 166–67: Thomas Vetter residence, Portland, OR; photo on p. 166 (top) courtesy Thomas Vetter.

pp. 56 (top), 153: Dan Liebowitz residence, Oakland, CA; designed by Jeni Webber.

pp. 57, 145: Dean Bates & Shirl Handley residence, Atlanta; designed by John Harper; photo p. 145 courtesy Dean Bates.

pp. 58–59: Brad & Nancy Lewis residence, Orinda, CA; designed by Michael Thilgen, Four Dimensions.

pp. 60 (top), 64, 75, 169, 185 (bottom right): Bill Renner residence, Oklahoma City.

pp. 62 (bottom), 63 (top): Carlo & Eulalie Scandiuzzi residence, Seattle; hardscape designed by Hendrikus Shraven; plantings designed by Keith Geller.

p. 63 (bottom): Tod Baker residence, Portland, OR.

p. 65 (right): Chris and Nita Ann Klein residence, Savannah, GA; designed by Jan S. Vandenbalck.

pp. 68–69, 163 (bottom): Grant & Arabelle Luckhardt residence, Atlanta; designed by Paula Refi; photo p. 68 (top) courtesy of Paula Refi.

pp. 70 (bottom), 100: Thomas B. Kirsch residence, Palo Alto, CA; designed by Bernard Trainor.

pp. 73, 158 (bottom): Bob & Delila Simon residence, Seattle; designed by Austin Heaton, Inc.

p. 76: Denver residence; designed by Clari Davis.

p. 78: Carl & Betty Romberg residence, Gainesville, GA.

pp. 80–81: Mark & Deborah Lyon residence, Mill Valley, CA; designed by Warren Simmonds.

p. 82 (top): Edie Thomas residence, Savannah, GA.

pp. 82 (bottom), 121: Hal & Caroline Silcox residence, Gainesville, GA.

p. 86 (top): Palo Alto, CA, residence; designed by Bernard Trainor.

pp. 86 (bottom), 136 (bottom), 156 (top): Don Schmidt residence, Cumming, GA; designed by John Mateyak.

p. 89: James & Stephanie Lindley residence, Savannah, GA.

pp. 91 (top), 129: Zaplin-Lampert Gallery, Santa Fe.

p. 91 (bottom): Sam Virgil, Jr. residence, Seattle.

p. 92 (bottom): David Thorne residence, Alameda, CA.

p. 93: Patrick Porter residence, Santa Fe.

p. 94 (bottom): Melinda Mullins residence, Santa Fe.

pp. 101 (bottom), 124–25: Gene & Marian Burch residence, Cumming, GA.

p. 103 (bottom): Mark Fockele residence, Gainesville, GA.

p. 106: Tama Fuller McGlynn residence, Atlanta.

p. 107 (right): Craig W. Thomsen property, Portland, OR.

p. 108 (top): Denver residence; designed by Colorado Design Group.

p. 108 (bottom): residences of Sam Virgil, Jr., Kelly Morse & Brian Custer, and Margot Andrzejensens, Seattle.

p. 109 (bottom): Wayland, MA, residence.

pp. 110, 132 (top): Selina & Bill Dwight residence, Palo Alto, CA; designed by Selina Dwight and Jeni Webber.

pp. 112 (bottom), 146, 180: Karen King residence, Atlanta; designed by Jeremey Smearman, Planters Nursery.

p. 114: Gary & Sue Homsey residence, Nichols Hills, OK; designed by Bill Renner.

pp. 116–117: Dave & Anne Hall residence, Seattle; photos pp. 116 and 117 (top) designed by Lisa Ravenholt.

p. 118: Boston residence; designed by Kevin Doyle.

pp. 119, 138: Oklahoma City residence; designed by Bill Renner.

pp. 123 (top), 147: Rosemary Kent residence, Palo Alto, CA; designed by Lawrence Booth.

p. 127: Alan & Lee Anne White residence, Cumming, GA.

pp. 130, 142: Ronald Cobb residence, Atlanta.

pp. 131, 154–55: David & Patricia Ketchum residence, Palo Alto, CA; designed by Jeni Webber.

p. 132 (bottom): Philip & Kate Zoercher residence, Gainesville, GA.

pp. 134-135: Betty Ajay residence, Bethel, CT.

p. 140: Sudbury, MA, residence; designed by Maria von Brincken.

p. 149: Michael & Susanne Snyder residence, Atlanta.

p. 151 (right): Marc & Rowena Singer residence, Oakland, CA; designed by Jeni Webber.

p. 160 (top): Perry & Brooke Thacker residence, Issaquah, WA.

p. 164: Andrew Schulman residence, Seattle.

p. 165: Brooks Garcia residence, Atlanta.

p. 170: Atlanta Botanical Garden.

pp. 173, 185 (bottom left): San Francisco residence; landscape design by Betsy Everdell; lighting design by Anna Kondolf.

p. 174: Gail Giffen residence, Lafayette, CA; designed by Michael Thilgen, Four Dimensions.

p. 175: Elizabeth Greenberg residence, San Rafael, CA; designed by Warren Simmonds.

pp. 176, 178, 182, 183: San Francisco residence; designed by Sonny Garcia; photo © Saxon Holt.

p. 179: Clari & Bob Davis residence, Denver.

p. 181: Pete & Mavin Howley, Mill Valley, CA; landscape design by Suzman Design Associates; lighting design by Anna Kondolf.